OPE
Northern
California

by Elizabeth Borsting

Open Road Travel Guides – designed for the
amount of time you *really* have for your trip!

Open Road Publishing

Open Road's new travel guides.
Designed to cut to the chase.
You don't need a huge travel encyclopedia – you need a *selective guide* to steer you right. If you're going on vacation for a few weeks or less, get a guide that brings you the *best* of any destination for the amount of time you *really* have for your trip!

Open Road – the guide you need for the trip you want.

The New Open Road *Best Of* Travel Guides.
Right to the point.
Uncluttered.
Easy.

Dedicated to my Best Traveling Companions –
Kurt, Jake, Katie and Ruby Jean

Open Road Publishing
P.O. Box 284, Cold Spring Harbor, NY 11724
www.openroadguides.com

Text Copyright © 2008 by Elizabeth Borsting
- All Rights Reserved -
ISBN 10: 1-59360-102-6
ISBN 13: 978-1-59360-102-7
Library of Congress Control No. 2007931962

For photo credits and About the Author, turn to page 239.

CONTENTS

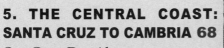

Maps

Open Road's Best Of
NORTHERN CALIFORNIA

1. INTRODUCTION

Northern California, from the Central Coast to the Bay Area and beyond, might very well be considered the state's crown jewel – elegant, but rarely ostentatious. This go-to guide will provide you with a portfolio of destinations worthy of your time.

Urbanites can sleuth the streets of **San Francisco** for the best shopping, dining and entertainment venues, while oenophiles can take a sideways journey to the **Wine Country** to search for the perfect pinot. For those who enjoy the great outdoors, there's plenty of open space to explore, from the rugged cliffs of **Big Sur** to the estuaries that dot the **Mendocino Coast** to a vigorous climb up Half Dome in **Yosemite National Park**. If historic sites and landmarks are more to your liking, there is the palatial (an understatement to say the least) Hearst Castle looming high atop a hill in lovely San Simeon. Let's not forget the Golden Gate Bridge, Tor House, Cannery Row and the marvelous missions that make California unique.

The region's coastline bears little resemblance to its sunny southern counterpart. The beaches north of Santa Barbara are rugged and chilly most of the year. Wide expanses of pebbled sand carve out tiny harbors where jutting pieces of jagged rock seem as if they're airbrushed. Most of the coastal towns are small, yet charming with clusters of restaurants, shops, galleries and wineries. Of course, there is always an exception and, in this case, it's **Santa Cruz,** laidback and often aglow with

sunshine. Its bustling seaside boardwalk is filled with rides, games and attractions. It's also home to the 1920s-era Giant Dipper, one of only two historic wooden roller coasters that still exist in the state.

If your plans call for a stay at a five-star wine country retreat, only the best have made the cut. If you prefer a more understated and elegant inn, those are listed, too. Should money be a concern, you'll also be pleased with those accommodations selected for the budget category. You'll feast on food and drink that originated from these parts—Cioppino, Crab Louis, martinis, the exotic Mai Tai, and Irish coffee. Maybe you'll snag a table at a culinary landmark, picnic among the vineyards, or graze on fresh Dungeness crab from a shack along San Francisco's Fisherman's Wharf. As for attractions, both the familiar and best-kept secrets have been included to help you plan an extraordinary itinerary.

This slim guide is plump with information. What you *won't* find is a clutter of unnecessary options. I've taken the liberty of deleting the ho-hum, giving you short, concise descriptions and itineraries that will assist you in planning a relaxing weekend getaway or, perhaps, a longer, more leisurely excursion. So, start packing – the best of Northern California awaits your arrival.

2. OVERVIEW

It's not unusual to assume that San Francisco represents the entire Northern California region. After all, we're accustomed to those images of fog clinging to the Golden Gate Bridge, the clang-clang of cable cars gliding along city streets, and people from all walks enjoying fresh Dungeness crab at some ramshackle kiosk near Fisherman's Wharf. But while this amazing city may be the region's epicenter, it doesn't by any means characterize the northern half of the state. In fact, once you venture beyond the city limits — whether you head north, south, or east — you'll discover destinations, both familiar and unknown, with their own distinct appeal.

You'll also find Northern California to be much more understated than its southern counterpart. People's interests are more grass roots rather than red carpets, and residents are apt to recycle, use public transportation, and rally for a good cause — be it political or social. Tinsel is strictly reserved for Christmas trees, and Klieg lights are more likely used, if at all, to direct you to a gallery opening rather than some movie premier. Even the coastline, with its craggy bluffs, sepia tone skyline, and pounding waves, bear little resemblance to any lyrics pulled from a Beach Boys song; instead, its desolate beauty has inspired the likes of Ansel Adams.

So, while San Francisco may be the pinnacle of Northern California, it is only one incredible slice of a much larger pie. This book has been sectioned into five separate destinations, which are briefly described on

10 Things to Plan Your Trip Around

• **Christmastime** in the Victorian Village of Ferndale.
• The return of the **Monarch Butterflies** to Pacific Grove in October.
• **Crab season** in San Francisco, mid-November through June, when devotees queue up along Fisherman's Wharf for the best of the catch.

• The tangy **Napa Valley Mustard Festival**, featuring an array of food, wine and art events in February and March.
• Paying homage to one of America's greatest writers at the **Steinbeck Festival** taking place each August in Monterey County.
• A chance to ward off vampires at the **Gilroy Garlic Festival** in July.
• Ringing in the **Chinese New Year** in February, a longstanding tradition in San Francisco.
• Doing a little toe-tapping at the **Monterey Jazz Festival** in September.
• The chance to ski Lake Tahoe's **Heavenly Resort**.
• An opportunity to go behind the kitchen door to whisk it up with culinary geniuses at the **Chefs' Holiday** event at the The Ahwahnee and Yosemite Lodge at the Falls at **Yosemite National Park**.

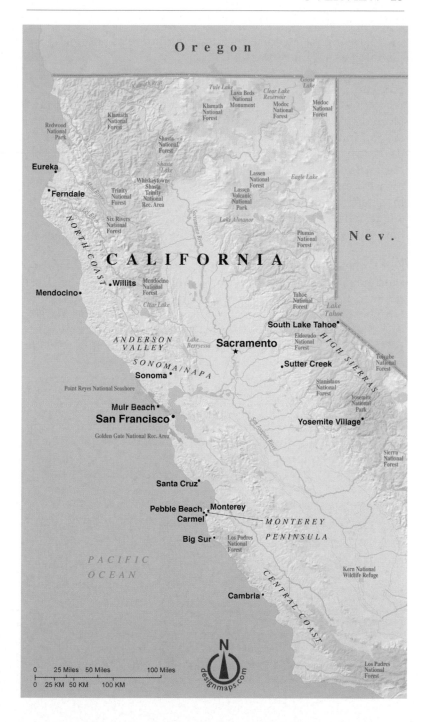

the following pages, to help gauge your interests and make the planning as simple as possible.

San Francisco

Sure, San Francisco is a major metropolis, but it's also a multi-faceted city composed of many neighborhoods. If you enjoy a taste of Italy, head to **North Beach** and its many trattorias.

Perhaps you have penchant for stylish boutiques, then traipse on over to **Union Street** in Cow Hollow. I've included the best and most interesting districts for you to spend time, as well as a suggested day trip to **Sausalito**, just a short ferry ride across the bay, where you can wander through art galleries and shops.

San Francisco truly has something for every traveler. There are museums, architectural offerings, fabulous shopping, and re-nowned hotels. As for restaurants and culinary pleasures, the city beckons the palette with its cache of casual to elegant eateries. The magnificent **Ferry Building Marketplace**, on its way to becoming an epicurean landmark, is filled with fabulous foods stalls representing the best the Bay Area has to offer.

The Wine Country: Napa & Sonoma

Located just a little more than an hour from San Francisco, California's bucolic Wine Country is a tangle of mostly tiny towns linked together by common corridors. The area is the union of two counties, **Napa** and **Sonoma**, and, like the varietals themselves, each area has its own palatable pleasures.

Napa is home to the **Silverado Trail**, Chef Thomas Keller's highly-acclaimed **French Laundry** restaurant, and the slow moving **Napa Wine Train**. Sonoma County, the larger of the two, is divided into three regions: the **Coasts and Sea Vil-**

lages, the **Rivers and Redwoods**, and the **Valleys and Vineyards**. No matter where you decide to hunker down, each region is intoxicating with their open spaces. The collection of tiny hamlets yields a mélange of tasting rooms, artisan cheese shops, gourmet grocers, stylish boutiques, and renowned bistros.

The Central Coast: From Santa Cruz to Cambria
Highway 1, at times as stomach-churning as any roller coaster, is a ribbon of roadway connecting some of the state's most spectacular scenery. The expanse of coastline, in all its rugged glory, is a series of jagged cliffs and long stretches of isolation. At the northern tip is **Santa Cruz**, a laidback surf ghetto with a decent share of sunshine and a seaside boardwalk full of amusements. As you travel south, the culture and climate dramatically change as you approach the **Monterey Peninsula, Carmel-by-the-Sea**, and **Big Sur**. This region boasts Victorian treasures, Hansel and Gretel architecture, and luxurious hilltop resorts that cater to famous guests. Further south is where you'll come upon **Hearst Castle** and the tiny town of **Cambria**, both enjoyable destinations.

High Sierras:
Yosemite & Lake Tahoe
Certainly one of the state's most photogenic areas, the High Sierra is one of Mother Nature's finest works. **Yosemite** and **Lake Tahoe**,

Best NoCal Restaurants

Northern California, especially San Francisco and the Wine Country, is known for its **fabulous restaurants**. Be sure to reserve a table at one of these dining destinations if you're in the area:

- **The Ahwahnee**, Yosemite National Park
- **Brambles Dinner House**, Cambria
- **Bouchée Restaurant & Wine Bar**, Carmel
- **Café Beaujolais**, Mendocino
- **Chez Panisse**, Berkeley (Bay Area)
- **Cielo at Ventana Inn**, Big Sur
- **Dry Creek Kitchen**, Healdsburg (Sonoma)
- **French Laundry**, Yountville (Napa)
- **Terra**, St. Helena (Napa)
- **The Slanted Door**, San Francisco

though aesthetically different, are both geological wonders. Yosemite National Park, the "Crown Jewel" of the nation's park system, is void of commercial clutter. With its jagged peaks and plunging valleys coupled with cascading waterfalls and hidden trails layered with beauty, it's truly eye candy for naturalists. Lake Tahoe (*see photo at left*) is equally stunning with its frosted peaks and placid lake. There's more of a vibe after dark with après-ski destinations, plush resorts, and casino action on the side of the lake belonging to Nevada.

The North Coast: Ferndale & Mendocino
The North Coast, a rugged and stunning coastal stretch, begins just past the Sonoma and trails upward towards the Oregon border. Its terrain, a mostly craggy coastline, is laden with desolate highways, giant redwood trees, and grazing elk skilled at ignoring the curious two-legged mammals prone to gawking in their presence. The region is home to **Ferndale**, an entire city designated an historic landmark by the state of California, and **Mendocino**, another vintage town set along the picturesque headlands. The North Coast is also home to the **Anderson Valley**, a 15-mile long winegrowing region less well known than Napa, but equally competitive when it comes to producing excellent wines.

Itineraries
If you've never been to Northern California, you'll want to be sure to take in the highlights, those "must-sees" and landmarks. If all you can spare is a weekend, choose an area and concentrate on the attractions in and around that destination.

Great places for a weekend jaunt include:
• San Francisco and Sausalito

Northern California's Best

• Enjoy a **Gourmet Picnic** at a Napa Valley Winery.
• Take the **Skunk Train** from Fort Bragg to Willits along the redwood-rimmed Noyo River in Mendocino County.
• Take a tour of **Hearst Castle** in San Simeon.
• Travel along **Highway 1** from Big Sur to Cambria.
• Do a little star gazing at **Yosemite National Park.**
• Strap on a pair of skis and hit the slopes of **Lake Tahoe.**
• Take a drive along the **Avenue of the Giants** while admiring 2,000 year old redwoods.
• Get out of the car and walk across San Francisco's **Golden Gate Bridge.**
• Get a real thrill with a ride aboard the **Giant Dipper Roller Coaster**, one of only two 1920s wooden seaside roller coasters left in the state, on the Santa Cruz Boardwalk.
• Watch the ferry boats arrive and depart for San Francisco from your jutting balcony at the **Inn Above Tide** in Sausalito.

• Sonoma and St. Helena
• The Monterey Peninsula
• Calistoga and Healdsburg
• Santa Cruz
• A secluded Big Sur resort
• A back-to-basics weekend in Yosemite
• Lake Tahoe's ski resorts

If you have an entire week to spend, you can fit in two regions, maybe three at the most.

Great places for a one-week trip include:
• San Francisco and Half Moon Bay
• San Francisco and The Wine Country
• The Wine Country and Mendocino
• The Central Coast: Monterey Peninsula, Big Sur and Cambria
• Mendocino and The Lost Coast/Ferndale
• San Francisco and Santa Cruz
• Yosemite and Lake Tahoe

Each destination chapter of this book guides you to the best sights in that region. Only you can decide what really piques your interest. So, take a look at what is presented; earmark those venues that sound the most appealing; and, finally, orchestrate a custom-made itinerary that works best for you.

3. SAN FRANCISCO

A pedestrian-friendly city often wrapped in folds of heavy fog, San Francisco measures a mere 49 square miles. And yet every vantage point seems to yield another famed landmark. Plant your feet atop **Nob Hill** where you'll catch a panorama of the **Golden Gate** and **Bay Bridges**, **Alcatraz Island** and **Coit Tower**, all visible in one sweeping, snapshot view. Still, not all of San Francisco's landmarks remain idle. The clang-clang of historic **cable cars** create a moveable feast for the eyes as passengers dangle from the sides before slipping from view into a fury of fog.

The city also offers a mosaic of ethnic and cultural destinations, from **North Beach** and its Italian influences to the dim sum restaurants of **Chinatown** to **Castro's** colorful gay ghetto. While prospectors may have settled the city, it's the "beat" generation and flower children from the Summer of Love whose imprints still remain instrumental in making San Francisco the fascinating place it is today.

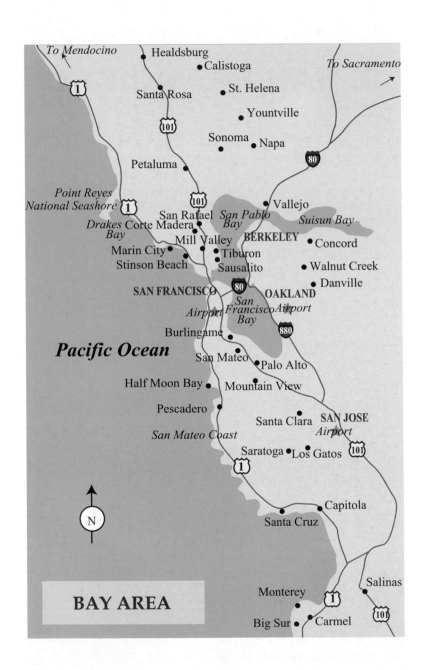

To Mendocino
Healdsburg
• Calistoga
To Sacramento
(1)
Santa Rosa
• St. Helena
• Yountville
(101)
Sonoma
• • Napa
Petaluma •
(80)
Point Reyes
National Seashore (1)
(101)
• Vallejo
San Rafael San Pablo
Drakes Corte Madera Bay
Bay
Suisun Bay
Mill Valley BERKELEY
• Concord
Marin City •
• Tiburon
Stinson Beach
Sausalito
• Walnut Creek
• Danville
SAN FRANCISCO (80) OAKLAND
San
Airport Francisco Airport
Bay
(880)
Burlingame •
Pacific Ocean
San Mateo •
• Palo Alto
Half Moon Bay •
Mountain View
Pescadero •
Santa Clara SAN JOSE
Airport
San Mateo Coast
Saratoga • Los Gatos (101)
(1)
N
• Capitola
Santa Cruz
Salinas
BAY AREA
Monterey (1)
Big Sur • Carmel (101)

ONE GREAT DAY IN SAN FRANCISCO

One day in San Francisco. Are you kidding? It's actually very doable, but you'll wish you had more time than a mere 24 hours. Forget about driving. Leave the car parked and take advantage of the excellent public transportation or, better yet, put on your most comfortable walking shoes and go exploring on two feet.

Begin the day with breakfast at **Boudin's Bakery** (see *Best Sleeps & Eats* chapter) at Fisherman's Wharf. Counter service at this restaurant/culinary shop offers signature sourdough bread, made-to-order breakfasts, and fresh-brewed **Peet's Coffee**. If the whether permits, dine outside on the patio.

Afterwards, explore the rest of **Fisherman's Wharf,** but keep your money in your wallet. The area is teeming with eager pitchmen trying to sell you tickets to some city tour or attraction, while the collection of souvenir shops teeter on tacky and tend to be overpriced. However, the no-frill grottos serving fresh clam chowder and seafood are worth trying. **Pier 39,**  a retail and dining complex, is also located along Fisherman's Wharf. Take a spin on the classic double-decker carousel, pose for a picture using Alcatraz Island as a backdrop, and pay a visit to the noisy sea lions who enjoy sunning themselves on the nearby docks.

From Pier 39, head to nearby **North Beach**. Here you'll find Columbus Street and neighboring avenues lined with espresso shops, outdoor cafes and trattorias, bakeries displaying home made canoli, and interesting stores. The famous **City Lights Bookstore** is at 261 Columbus, where writers from the Beat Generation, including Jack Kerouac, gathered for literary discussions.

Next head east toward the **Embarcadero**, once again brushing past Fisherman's Wharf. It's an interesting walk as you pass the piers where ships of all flags are sheltered. At the foot of Market Street is the fabulous 1898 **Ferry Building**, which received a new lease on life when it was transformed into a vibrant public food hall boasting high-end retailers, delightful restaurants, and a farmers market held every Tuesday and Saturday. The striking clock tower is a beacon for gourmands who scurry in and out in search of organic mushrooms, oysters plucked fresh from the sea, hand-pressed olive oil, and other delicacies. This is where you can also catch the ferry to the charming village of Sausalito, as well as other waterfront towns in Marin County. Personally, the Ferry Building Marketplace is one of my favorite San Francisco stops, and you can grab a quick lunch here at one of the many cafes, bistros or counter-only eateries.

Walk out the front door of the **Ferry Building Marketplace** to Market Street. Continue along Market Street brushing past the **Financial District** towards **Union Square**. When you get to Powell Street, where the cable car turnaround is located across from

Ride a Historic Streetcar

San Francisco is famous for its historic cable cars, but you can also travel back in time on a collection of **historic streetcars**, which have offered regular service to residents and visitors for more than a decade. These beautiful streetcars are each painted in its original livery and once graced the streets of Boston, Chicago or Milan. They run along the center of Market Street between the Castro District and Fisherman's Wharf and are collectively known as line **F-Line**.

Nordstrom, that's when you've arrived to this shopping mecca. On some days, most days actually, it's elbow-to-elbow on the narrow sidewalks as shoppers dart in and out of H&M, Macy's, Neiman Marcus, and Williams-Sonoma, as well as high end places like Hermès of Paris, Frette and Gucci. The landmark park offers a fabulous resting spot with its granite plaza and original sculptures.

Just off Union Square, between Kearney and Stockton Streets, is **Maiden Lane**. This pedestrian-only alleyway, with its soaring iron gates marking its entrance, is somewhat hidden. During the Barbary Coast era this was a red-light district, then known as Morton Street, that reported at least one murder a week. The brothels were destroyed after the 1906 fire and the street was then rechristened to its present name. It's a trendy little two-block stretch with unique boutiques and restaurants peppered with espresso-drinking shoppers who stop to relax at one of the sidewalk cafes.

From Union Square and Maiden Lane make your way up to **Chinatown**. The entrance to Chinatown, which is the largest and oldest Chinatown outside of Asia, is marked by the imposing dragon gate at Grant Avenue and Bush Street. As you step through the gateway it feels as if you're really entering a different world as the street is flanked with dragon-entwined lampposts, street signs written in both English and Chinese, and swaying paper lanterns. The sound of clicking mahjongg tiles resonates from behind shrouded windows, and the smell of exotic herbs can also be detected.

As you wander down **Grant Av-**

San Francisco Bay

Marina Green

Museo Italo-Americano

Casa Way
Rico
Buchanan
Cervantes Blvd
Mallorca Way

Jefferson
Beach St
North Point
Bay St

SF Craft & Folk Art Mus.

Fort Mason

Mexican Mus.

Aquatic Park

S.F. Maritime National Historic Park

Maritime Museum

Ghirardelli Square

45   43 1/2 43   41   Pier 39
47
Ferries to Angel Island Sausalito Tiburon Alcatraz

Jefferson St
The Cannery
Beach St

North Point

Underwater World

FISHERMAN'S WHARF

Stockton St

Moscone Rec. Center

Toledo
MARINA
101   Lombard St

Francisco St

Russian Hill Park

Bay St
Francisco St
Columbus Ave

Chestnut St
Library North Beach Playground

Alice Marble Tennis Courts

Lombard St
Greenwich St
Sts. Peter & Paul
Washington Square

Hyde St
Leavenworth St
Filbert St
Union St

COW HOLLOW

Union St
Green St
Pierce St
Steiner St
Fillmore St
Webster St
Laguna St
Octavia St
Gough St

Franklin St
Van Ness Ave
Polk St
Larkin St

Green St
Vallejo St
Jones St
Taylor St
Mason St
Powell St

Broadway Tunnel

Pacific Ave
Jackson St
Washington St

RUSSIAN HILL
Cable Car Line

PACIFIC HEIGHTS

Alta Plaza Park

California Pacific Medical Center

Lafayette Park

Octavia St

Clay St
Sacramento St
Cable Car Line
California St

Grace Cathedral

Huntington Park

California St

Pine St
Bush St

St. Francis Hospital

NOB HILL

Jones St
Mason St

Sutter St
Post St

JAPANTOWN

Japan Center

St. Mary's Cathedral

Geary St
O'Farrell St
Ellis St
Eddy St

Hyde St
Leavenworth St
Taylor St

Hamilton Rec. Center
Geary Expwy

101

Kimball Playground

WESTERN ADDITION

Ellis St
Eddy St
Scott St
Pierce St
Steiner St
Fillmore St
Webster St
Laguna St

Jefferson Square

Hayward Playground

McAllister St

Polk St
Larkin St
Van Ness Ave
Franklin St

Turk St
Eddy St

Federal Building
State Building
War Mem. Opera House

Golden Gate Ave
Asian Art Museum
Civic Center Plaza
City Hall
Brooks Hall

MUNI Metro
BART

U.N. Plaza
Fulton St
Library

7th St
8th St
Mission St
9th St

BART/ Muni Sta.

Civic Center Station

Howard St

Divisadero St
Broderick St

Alamo Square

Fulton St
Grove St
Hayes St

Buchanan St
Gough St

Bill Graham Civic Auditorium

Davies Symphony Hall

Fell St
Oak St
HAYES VALLEY

Muni Sta.

Van Ness Station

10th St
11th St

Page St

Pierce St

LOWER HAIGHT

Haight St
Waller St
UC Extension

Octavia St
Market St
Van Ness Ave

McCoppin St

S. Van Ness Ave

12th St

Hermann St
US Mint

Buena Vista Park

Lloyd St
Duboce Park

Castro

Davies Medical Center

Duboce Ave

Church St
Steiner

Mission St

Duboce Ave (under)
101

14th St

10th St

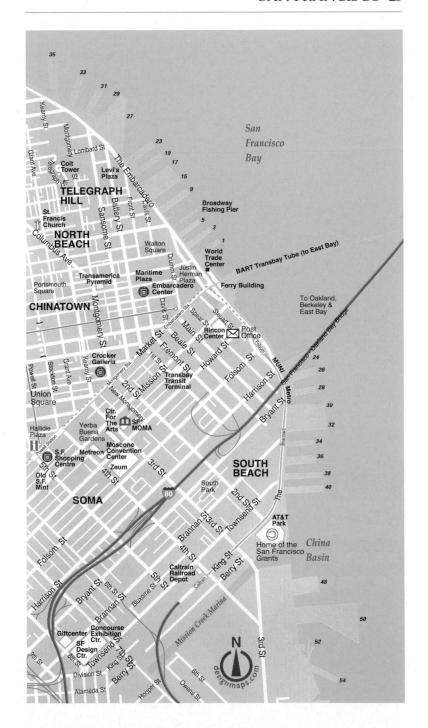

enue, you'll pass by a number of kitschy shops that once housed more authentic wares. Still, you can prowl for silk pajamas, tea sets, herbs and fancy chopsticks. I bought my 4-year-old daughter a darling Chinese dress — or *Cheongsam* — for a song. Between Jackson and Washington streets is Ross Alley where the **Golden Gate Fortune Cookie Company** is located at 52 Ross Alley. Opened in 1962, it is the only fortune cookie company left in Chinatown and, although productive, seems as if it is as much of a tourist attraction as it is a cookie factory. Get a firsthand look at how these post-meal morsels are made with a simple hot press and a steel rod that is used to mold the dough into its trademark crescent shape.

ALTERNATIVE PLAN
Forget the dim sum and bid farewell to Chinatown. Instead, head back to **Nob Hill** on the cable car and pop into the **Top of the Mark**, situated on the 19th floor of the storied Mark Hopkins Hotel. Spend the evening listening to live jazz (most nights), savoring a stiff martini and marveling at some rather remarkable city views. *Info*: 999 California Street. Tel. 415/392-3434. www.sanfrancisco.intercontinental.com.

After prowling around the Chinatown shops, stop for dinner at one of the authentic dim sum restaurants. These are not fancy restaurants by any stretch of the imagination, but the food and service are good. **Hang Ah Tea Room** is tucked away at the end of a small alley and is one of Chinatown's oldest dim sum eateries. The interiors are awash in yellow and green accents and the clientele is a mix of locals and fortunate tourists. It's also great for kids. *Info*: 1 Pagoda Place. Tel. 415/956-2902.

A FANTASTIC SAN FRANCISCO WEEKEND

A **weekend** in San Francisco is romantic, exhilarating, delicious and unforgettable. Its hilly landscape and constant veil of fog, coupled with fabulous shopping, eye-popping landmarks, epicurean offerings and eclectic neighborhoods, all contribute to what will likely be the most memorable 72 hours of your life.

Friday Evening
Check in to a classic San Francisco hotel. My first pick would be **The Fairmont San Francisco** atop Nob Hill (also known as "Snob Hill"). It's a fabulous historic property with a great location that's convenient to the cable car line. It's also expensive, so my other choice would be the more budget-friendly **Kensington Park Hotel** just off Union Square. This too is a great property near the Powell-Mason Cable Car Line and a plethora of great shops, restaurants and the Theater District. For more details on both properties, flip to the *Best Sleeps & Eats* chapter.

Hop aboard the **Powell-Hyde Cable Car** line near the Powell Market turnaround or somewhere along Powell Street near Union Square. You can also catch the cable car further up near the Fairmont Hotel. Take the line to Fisherman's Wharf, disembarking at the turnaround where the line terminates. Begin the evening by stopping into the **Buena Vista** at the corner of Hyde and Beach. Belly up to the bar and order an Irish Coffee, which was invented on the premises in 1952.

Now head over to nearby North Beach to see *Beach Blanket Babylon*, the longest running musical in history. This zany musical spoofs pop culture and, after more than three decades, it has become a San Francisco institution and must-see for first-time visitors. It's often sold out weeks in advance, so plan accordingly. Tickets start at just $25 per person. *Info*: www.beachblanketbabylon.com. Tel. 415/421-4222. North Beach. At Club Fugazi, 678 Beach Blanket Babylon Boulevard (Green Street).

SF's Culinary Firsts

San Francisco is known for many things, including its culinary offerings. In fact, the following were **invented, introduced or first ingested** in the City by the Bay:

- Green Goddess Salad Dressing
- Cioppino
- The Popsicle
- The Martini
- Irish Coffee
- Crab Louis
- Mai Tais

The city can also be credited with helping to start such food trends as Asian fusion, exotic greens, heirloom tomatoes and pedigree produce. Who knew?

San Francisco for Free!

Go ahead and leave your heart in San Francisco, but don't leave your hard earned cash. There are plenty of things to do and see that won't cost you a nickel.

• Take a 1.7 mile walk (3.4 miles roundtrip) across the **Golden Gate Bridge** and enjoy endless photo opportunities along the way.

• Head to **Pier 39** to get an up-close and personal look at the throngs of seals sunning themselves on the docks; then take in a free show from a street performer.

• Tour the first floor murals at **Coit Tower**.

• Take a tour of the **Cable Car Barn and Powerhouse,** a fascinating museum providing the history and little known facts of the city's moving landmarks.

• Admire San Francisco's "Painted Ladies" at **Alamo Square**, where you'll witness a breathtaking row of Victorian houses. Bring a picnic lunch and bask in the beauty.

• Do a little toe tapping at the **Golden Gate Park Band Concerts** on the lawn near the San Francisco Botanical Garden, every Sunday at 1pm from April-October.

• Get a bird's eye view of the city by boarding one of five outdoor Otis glass elevators at the **Westin St. Francis** in Union Square. Press button "32" and watch the city unfold before your eyes as you ascend at a brisk speed of 1000 feet per minute.

• Take a zig-zagged saunter down **Lombard Street** (*see photo below*), better known as the Crookedest Street in the World, from atop Russian Hill at Hyde Street.

• See how the classic fortune cookie is made at the

Golden Gate Fortune Cookie Company in Chinatown.

• Take a docent-led walking tour of different parts of the city with **San Francisco City Guides**, a non-profit organization boasting more than 200 trained volunteers.

After the show, head to a North Beach café, such as **Washington Square Bar & Grill** (www.wsbg.ypguides.net. Tel. 415/982-8123. North Beach/Washington Square. 1707 Powell Street at Union) for a nightcap and some live jazz. Or take a stroll up Columbus Avenue and find an empty table at one of the many espresso bars and trattorias. When you're ready to go home, hail a cab or make your way to the **Powell-Mason Cable** Car line, which you can pick up along Columbus Avenue. It will take you back to Nob Hill and Union Square. Fall asleep listening to the sounds of the city. Before you know it, you'll hear the faint clang of the cable car bell as it makes it first run of the day.

Saturday

Today let's explore some of San Francisco's unique neighborhoods. Start by having breakfast either at your hotel or in the nearby vicinity. A nice place to grab a quick bite is at **Emporio Rulli**, a European-style café offering pastries and coffee on the plaza in Union Square. You can stake claim to an outdoor table and enjoy the morning scenery as it unfolds with passengers hanging from the cable cars and determined shoppers darting in and out of tony shops. If you think you might want to see a show while you're in town, **TIX**, the half-price ticket booth, is located in the plaza as well. Check out to see what play or musical might have available seats for a fraction of the price.

While tourists are notably drawn to Union Square and Chinatown, it's the residential neighborhoods that are really the most colorful. Most districts have their own little villages brimming with shops, restaurants and a cast of characters that actually dwell in nearby flats. My two favorite neighborhoods are **Cow Hollow** and **The**

ALTERNATIVE PLAN

Maybe it's been a long day, you've had a long flight, and exploring the town just isn't in the cards. If that's the case, then head to **Harry Denton's Starlight Room** atop the Sir Francis Drake Hotel. This rooftop nightclub sits 21 stories high and offers panoramic city views, thirst-quenching cocktails, light meals, and dancing to live music until 2am if you feel so inclined. It's a throwback to a more glamorous age but with a modern-day twist. *Info*: www.harrydenton.com. Tel. 415/395-8595. Union Square. 450 Powell St.

Take MUNI

The best way to get around San Francisco is the San Francisco Municipal Transportation Agency, better known as **MUNI**, which includes city buses, historic streetcars, cable cars, trolley cars, and light rail vehicles. **Visitor Passports**, good for one, three or seven days, are well worth the money considering it costs $5 just to take a single, one-way ride on a cable car. You can purchase a Visitor Passport at the cable car ticket booth at Beach & Hyde near Fisherman's Wharf or at the San Francisco Airport. *Info*: For a complete list of bus routes and vendor locations where you can purchase Visitor Passports, go to www.sfmta.com.

Marina, both of which can be enjoyed in the same visit. Cow Hollow is an affluent neighborhood located between Russian Hill and The Presidio bordering both The Marina and Pacific Heights. Its name comes from the cows that once grazed on the land, but now it's bursting with well-heeled urbanites who do a little of their own grazing at some very hip restaurants along **Union Street**, the main thoroughfare contained between Van Ness and Steiner.

Near the beginning of Cow Hollow, near the intersection of Union and Gough Streets, is the **Octagon House**, an eight-sided, blue-hued abode built in 1861 that now pays homage to early American history. Inside are Revolutionary War playing cards whose deck contains no kings, queens or jacks, the original signatures from 54 of the 56 men who signed the Declaration of Independence, and antique furniture dating back to the 18th and 19th centuries. *Info*: Tel. 415/441-7512. Cow Hollow. 2645 Gough Street. Informal tours are conducted the second Sunday and second and fourth Thursdays from noon-3pm. Closed January and holidays. Free.

As you make your way down **Union Street**, you'll want to stop at many of the fascinating art galleries and one-of-a-kind shops that are housed inside original Victorian structures. There are also some charming cafes and coffeehouses to grab a snack or beverage. You'll also find everything from rice-paper lamps to vintage timepieces to chunks of organic soap available for purchase. If you're visiting in June, the street closes to vehicular traffic for the **Union Street Arts Festival** featuring live music, street performers, arts and crafts booths, a race between restaurant waiters and lots more. Admission is free.

Near the corner of Union and Webster Streets is the **Vendanta Temple**, which many claim to be among the city's most unique edifices. Built around 1905, the structure is an amalgam of architectural influences, including Colonial, Queen Anne, Moorish and Hindu. *Info*: Cow Hollow. 2963 Webster Street. Visit www.unionstreet.com for more information on the entire area.

From Union Street, make your way down to **The Marina** on foot via Fillmore Street. It's a somewhat interesting walk and, thankfully, downhill too. Within about 20 minutes you'll arrive at **Chestnut Street**, an eclectic mix of shops, restaurants, and coffeehouses. There is a great neighborhood vibe taking place along Chestnut, and the weekly **Farmers' Market**, held Saturdays from 10am-2pm May through October at the local middle school on Fillmore, is a great place to mingle with the locals.

It's often said that the best Italian food is found in North Beach, but **Lucca Delicatessen** is one of the city's most celebrated Italian delis. The snug space is loaded with bottles of olive oil and balsamic vinaigrette offset by rows of salami suspended from above. If you're feeling hunger pangs at this point, you may want to pop in and order one of their monster-size deli sandwiches. *Info*: www.luccadeli.com. Tel. 415/921-7873. The Marina. 2120 Chestnut St.

After you do some window shopping — or some serious spending — head to **Golden Gate Park**, a rectangular greenbelt that is larger than New York City's Central Park. You can either arrive on the MUNI, which will require at least one transfer, or you can hop a cab. Created from land that was nothing more

than sand dunes, the park boasts some one million trees, a placid lake and ponds, and even its own paddock filled with buffalo.

You won't be able to see everything in one visit, but one of your first stops should be to the **Conservatory of Flowers** established in 1879 (*see photo on previous page*). In 1995 the glass and wood Victorian greenhouse, the oldest such structure in the Western hemisphere, was damaged by a severe storm and closed for nearly a decade. It finally reopened in 2003 after a $25 million restoration. Check out the east wing where giant lily pads tread water and are sturdy enough to hold the weight of a toddler-size child. Be sure to take in the cityscapes created from flowers out front. *Info*: www.conservatoryofflowers.com. Tel. 415/666-7001. Golden Gate Park. 501 Stanyan Street. Closed Monday. Admission: $5 adults, $1.50 children.

Next, head to the **M.H.de Young Museum**, founded in 1895 and, since 2005, housed in a spectacular state-of-the-art facility that integrates art, architecture and the natural landscape. Inside is a diverse collection of American paintings and decoratve arts coupled with arts of the Americas, the Pacific Islands, and Africa. If you're not up to doing a little gallery slumming, then relax among the gardens which are free to the public. On Saturdays from 10:30am to noon there are kids' programs; no reservations are required. *Info*: www.deyoungmuseum.org. Tel. 415-750-3528.

Golden Gate Park. 50 Hagiwara Tea Garden Drive. $10 adults, $6 ages 13-17, under 12 free.

Now wander next door to the **Japanese Tea Garden**, one of the city's most peaceful attractions. A Golden Gate Park fixture since 1894 and the oldest public Japanese Garden in the nation, it's an ideal place to enjoy a Zen-like cup of tea while admiring the serene waters. Boasting five landscaped acres, the garden is punctuated by arched bridges, rambling

Golden Gate Park Freebies

• Take a free guided walk through the **San Francisco Botanical Garden** at Strybing Arboretum.

• Cut a rug, or some grass, every Sunday from 11am-1:30pm when **swing dancers** gather at JFK Drive between 9th and 10th Avenues to sway the afternoon away.

• Test your knowledge of English literature by naming as many flowers and plants as you can from Bard's poems and plays found in the **Garden of Shakespeare's Flowers**.

• Watch the **model boats** dart back and forth across Spreckels Lake at Kennedy Drive and 35th Avenue.

• Enjoy a sobering moment with a visit to the **AIDS Memorial Grove** at Bowling Green Drive and Middle Drive East.

• Head to the Music Concourse for a **free Sunday concert** in the park. The Golden Gate Park Band has performed here continuously since 1882.

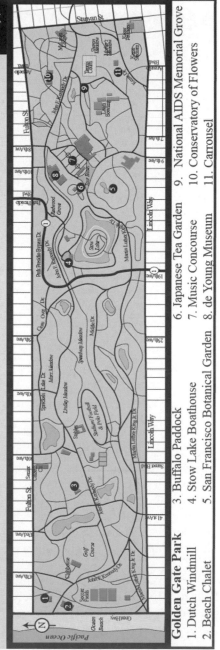

Golden Gate Park
1. Dutch Windmill
2. Beach Chalet
3. Buffalo Paddock
4. Stow Lake Boathouse
5. San Francisco Botanical Garden
6. Japanese Tea Garden
7. Music Concourse
8. de Young Museum
9. National AIDS Memorial Grove
10. Conservatory of Flowers
11. Carrousel

> **ALTERNATIVE PLAN**
> More in the mood for a fine dinner and a first-run play? Head to the **Tenderloin District**, a 20-square block area west of Union Square and home to what some refer to, but not the locals, as the Theatre District. Have dinner at **Asia de Cuba** inside the Clift Hotel for innovative Asian-Latin cuisine. Then take in a show – perhaps the **American Conservatory Theater** at the Geary Theater, or the **San Francisco Opera House** on the neighborhood's western edge, or more experimental entertainment, such as the **EXIT Theatre**, which occupies four storefront theaters yielding various productions. There is also a number of jazz and blues clubs, some 200 restaurants and cafes, and a lion's share of dive bars.

streams, graceful waterfalls, renowned sculptures, traditional Japanese architecture, and a beautiful tea house.

After leaving Golden Gate Park, head to the former hippie haven of **Haight-Ashbury**, which borders the park to the southeast. There's still that Summer of Love feel of the counter culture '60s with traces of flower power and the occasional faint scent of burning incense. These days there are more high-end boutiques and Internet cafes than there are head shops. If you're a fan of the **Grateful Dead,** take a look at **710 Ashbury Street** where the legendary musical group once lived. Not far from here, at **112 Lyon Street**, is where hippie chic **Janice Joplin** dwelled.

If you like to shop, there are a number of unusual offerings along **Haight Street**, including independent bookstores, art galleries and more (see Chapter 10, *Best Activities*, for more details). For an insiders look at The Haight District, take the **Haight Ashbury Flower Power Walking Tour**, where you'll discover the area's rich history, Victorian charm and stories from the psychedelic decade. *Info*: www.haightashburytour.com. Tel. 415/863-1621.

After you've done a little tripping through The Haight, why not stay for dinner? Head to the widely popular **Cha! Cha! Cha!** With its electric blue edifice and crimson red doors, this Caribbean eatery is easy to spot. *Info*: 1801 Haight Street. Tel. 415/386-5758.

Sunday
It's your final day in the city, so you'll want to make the most of it. Start your morning with an uplifting sermon at the **Glide Memorial Church** where you'll hear a sermon on social justice and while rocking out to the infectious sounds of the **Glide Ensemble**, the 100-plus choir that brings the entire congregation to its feet with heartfelt clapping, swaying and a thunderous repertoire of gospel music. Even if you have no religious affiliation, a Sunday morning at The Glide is something worth experiencing. Services start at 9am and end around 11am. Arrive about 30 minutes prior to secure a seat. Otherwise, it's standing room only. *Info*: www.glide.org. Tel. 415/674-6090. Tenderloin. 330 Ellis Street.

Next, you'll want to make your way to **SoMa,** which stands for South of Market. This two-square mile area is full of shopping outlets and art galleries, as well as great nightclubs and some experimental theaters. Plan on spending some time at the **San Francisco Museum of Modern Art** located at Third and Howard Streets. Inside are more than 15,000 works of art representing all mediums, from painting and sculpture to architecture and design. *Info*: www.sfmoma.org. Tel. 415/357-4000. SoMa. 151 Third Street. Closed Wednesday. Admission: $12.50 adults, 12 and under free.

Next, stroll on over to the **Yerba Buena Gardens**, a public park that spans two city blocks between Third and Fourth, Mission and Folsom Streets.

A pedestrian bridge suspended above Howard Street connects the two blocks. This is a great place to visit, especially with kids or if you just want to feel like a kid yourself. The rooftop of the gardens, which partially covers the **Moscone Center,** features a playground, the original 1906 Looff Carousel that once graced the city's long-forgotten Playland-at-the-Beach, an interactive museum, an ice skating rink and bowling center.

ALTERNATIVE PLAN

If you're not much of a Giants fan (keep that to yourself while in this city) then you may want to visit **The Museum of the African Diaspora** at Third and Mission Streets. The face of a child composed of some 2,100 images beckons visitors, where a plethora of exhibits showcase African experiences in both San Francisco and around the globe. *Info*: www.moadsf.com. Tel. 415/358-7200. SoMa. 685 Mission Street at Third. $10 adults. $5 students. 12 and under free.

Nearby is a playground flanked with tunnel slides, a spongy rubber floor and splashing fountain. The **Zeum**, a high-tech museum for older kids which allows them to create animated videos, is also found here.

AT&T Park, touted as the "Miracle on Third Street," is home to the San Francisco Giants. **Guided Insider's Tours**, taking you to areas only privy to players and staff, are offered daily at 10:30am and 12:30pm. Here's your chance to sit in the dugout, experience a big league clubhouse, stroll out onto the field, and visit other places not normally viewed by the public. *Info*: www.sanfranciscogiants.mlb.com. Tel. 415/972-2212. $10 adults, $6 children.

From SoMa, make your way back to Market Street and head right towards the **Embarcadero**. At the foot of Market Street is, as mentioned before in this chapter, the **Ferry Building Marketplace** and its throng of culinary shops, restaurants and eateries. Your best bet would be to grab a bite here. My recommendations would be **Lulu Petite** for gourmet sandwiches, Vietnamese specialties from **Out the Door** (part of the Slanted Door family), or the upscale **Market Bar** if time allows. See Chapter 9, *Best Sleeps & Eats*, for details.

Next head to Pier 33 along The Embarcadero near the intersection of Bay Street to board the evening ferry to **Alcatraz Island**. Tickets must be purchased in advance, so I advise doing this as soon as possible as tours sell out quickly – especially on weekends. Don't forget to dress warmly as it gets chilly after sundown regardless of the season.

The evening tour gives visitors a more interesting perspective of what life on Alcatraz must have been like for both the prisoners and the security guards who lived on  The Rock with their families and young children. The evening ferry ride to Alcatraz circles the island and the captain gives a live narration about its history.

Upon docking, you'll get a guided tour from the dock to the cellhouse level where the audio tour begins. Narrated by former prisoners and guards, the tour is at times gripping and really brings the history of Alcatraz to life. You'll take the tour at your own pace and, on average, plan on about spending 2 1/2 hours exploring the cellhouse and surrounding grounds. Famous events, such as escape attempts, food riots, and life behind the steel doors of solitary confinement, are told in great detail.

ALERNATIVE PLAN
Go to **Bistro Boudin** at Fisherman's Wharf (see *Best Sleeps & Eats* chapter). You can take the free **Museum & Bakery Tour** after your meal, which showcases a collection of historic and interactive exhibits. You'll also see the bakery in full swing from the museum's floor-to-ceiling window walls and transparent catwalk. *Info*: www.boudinbakery.com. Tel. 415.928.1849. Fisherman's Wharf. 160 Jefferson.

No one ever escaped The Rock, though some 36 prisoners were involved in 14 separate escape attempts. Twenty-three were caught, a half-dozen shot and killed, and two drowned. Five men disappeared and their whereabouts are still unknown, but they were assumed drowned. *Info*: www.alcatrazcruises.com. Tel. 415/981-7625. The Embarcadero – Pier 33. Night Tour is offered Thursday-Monday.

$31.50 per person – this is for the ferry ride. Alcatraz is operated by the National Park Service, Department of the Interior.

A WONDERFUL WEEK IN THE BAY AREA

With an entire week to spend in San Francisco, you'll wander through prestigious museums and landmarks, take a leisurely walk across the Golden Gate Bridge, spend some time visiting the attractions at **Golden Gate Park**, do some shopping along **Union Square,** take a neighborhood walking tour, and venture across the bay to the charming seaside village of **Sausalito**. When the stomach starts growling, be sure to check out my favorite restaurants in the San Francisco section of the *Best Sleep & Eats* chapter.

RECOMMENDED PLAN: Spend five days in San Francisco exploring all the unique neighborhoods and attractions found in the *One Great Day* and *A Fantastic Weekend* sections, along with additional off-beat neighborhoods detailed below. Spend a good part of one day in **Sausalito**, just across the bay from the city, and then head to **Half Moon Bay** for an unexpected getaway. Don't forget to leave a day open to prowl the city's extraordinary museums.

Japantown
Located about a mile west of Union Square is **Japantown**. The area's heart and soul is found at **Japan Center**, a five-acre complex brimming with hotels, shops, theaters, sushi bars and restaurants at the intersection of Post and Buchanan Streets. It is easily recognizable by its five-tiered pagoda, a gift from the Japanese government and a symbol of eternal peace. The **Webster Bridge**, located midway in the center, ironically evokes the Ponte Vecchio in Florence, Italy.

Head to **Nihonmachi Mall**, a pedestrian area lined with an array of eclectic shops, designed to look like a traditional Japanese village. Its centerpiece, stunning cast bronze fountains by Ruth Asawa, grace the landscape. If you wander over to **Bush Street** you'll notice food and flowers lining **The Konko Kyo Temple's** fine wood altar. These offerings are left by residents throughout the day.

There are plenty of shopping opportunities in Japantown, and you'll find everything from clothing, books, furniture, and jewelry, just to name a few. **Kinokuniya Stationery** (T. 415/567-8901, 1581 Webster Street) boasts A great way to conclude your

> ### Don't Miss ...
>
> • A chance to walk across the **Golden Gate Bridge**.
> • A nighttime tour of **Alcatraz**.
> • A visit to the **Ferry Building Marketplace** to sample its culinary offerings.
> • A drink at **The Top of the Mark** inside the Mark Hopkins Hotel.
> • A ride aboard a **landmark cable car**.
> • Hanging out in **North Beach**.
> • Sipping Irish coffee inside the **Buena Vista** near Fisherman's Wharf.

visit to Japantown is to head an impressive collection of decorative papers, pens, stationery and unusual items for yourself or to give to someone else. If you enjoy Japanese literature, periodicals or comic books, **Kinokuniya Bookstore** (Tel. 415/567-3524, 1581 Webster St.) offers hundreds of titles with a handful printed in English. For a little pick-me-up, head to **Kabuki Springs and Spa** (Tel. 415/922-6000, 1750 Geary Blvd. at Fillmore) where you can soak in traditional Japanese-style communal baths and enjoy an authentic shiatsu massage.

At the intersection of Sutter and Buchannan, just outside the mall, is where you'll happen upon the **Japanese Cultural and Community Center**. This the epicenter for art exhibitions, film screenings and the plight of the Japanese American community. Should you want to submerse yourself in the culture, pay a visit to the **Soto Zen Mission Sokoji Buddhist Temple** at Laguna and Sutter. It is one of five churches in the area serving Japanese residents from the city and outlying areas.

Sushi, Anyone?

In the mood for some succulent sushi or traditional Japanese fare? You'll find plenty of restaurants within Japan Center, as well as along Post Street and within the Buchanan Mall. Check out **Isobune** in Kintetsu Mall (Tel. 415/563-1030, 1737 Post Street), where wooden boats float by and sushi addicts simply pluck pieces of seaweed wrapped morsels from the slow-moving vessels.

to the **Asian Art Museum** near the **Civic Center**. Redesigned by Italian architect Gae Aulenti, the museum features a trio of floors that house collection galleries with more than 15,000 objects spanning some 6,000 years. Jade, stone and bronze sculptures are found along with paintings, scrolls, furniture, armor and even puppets. A stunning slit glass ceiling invites the sunlight to pour through illuminating the museum's grand staircase. *Info*: www.asianart.org, Tel. 415/581-3500. Downtown. 200 Larkin Street. Open Tuesday-Sunday 10am-5pm until 9pm on Thursday. Adults $12, 12 and under free.

If you happen to be visiting in April, Japantown goes all out to celebrate its **Cherry Blossom Festival**. Among the many lively happenings are Taiko drumming, martial arts, doll-making and calligraphy demonstrations plus a very vibrant parade to mark the occasion.

Angel Island
San Francisco's Asian history is fascinating and ventures beyond the city's ethnic neighborhoods. You may want to make **Angel Island**, often referred to as the "Ellis Island of the West," your main focus and visit Japantown and Chinatown on another day. You'll catch the Blue and Gold Fleet ferry at Pier 39 (plan ahead as service is limited) and sail to the middle of the bay where the 740-acre island is located. A guided tour illustrates Angel Island's rich history as a Civil War encampment, a quarantine station, a POW camp, a missile base, and an immigration station where 250,000 Chinese immigrants were processed with an average detention of two weeks. An old barracks, once known as China

Cove, has been preserved. Segway tours of the island are also available. *Info*: www.blueandgoldfleet.com. Tel. 415/705-8200.

The Castro District
What once were dirt roads and productive dairy farms is now a rainbow of imaginative boutiques, bookstores, and bars. The Castro is the epicenter of San Francisco's gay community and one of the more colorful corners of town.

While you don't have to be straight to venture to such places as Fisherman's Wharf or Union Square, the same is true for exploring The Castro – you don't have to be gay or lesbian. All you need is an open mind. There is some interesting history within these blocks, including the **Harvey Milk Plaza** at Market and Castro, which pays homage to the city's slain gay rights leader. Milk, the city's first openly gay supervisor, along with Mayor George Moscone, was assassinated in 1978 by fellow supervisor Dan White. Nearby is **Pink Triangle Park**, just behind the City Athletic Club, which honors the memories of the many thousands of homosexuals who were victims of the Holocaust.

The historic **Castro Theatre,** built in 1922, is a testament to the movie palaces of yesteryear. It is one of the few remaining movie palaces in the nation that is still in operation. No matter what's displayed on the marquee—the latest blockbuster movie or a classic silent film—just hearing the sounds of the Mighty Wurlitzer Organ is worth the price of admission.  The interiors are lavish, combining Art Deco elegance with Moorish influences. *Info*: www.thecastrotheatre.com. Tel. 415/621-6120. 429 Castro St.

CityPass & Go Cards

If you're spending a week in San Francisco, get the **San Francisco CityPass**. For $54 adults, $39 children, you'll be privy to admission to some half-dozen attractions, including the Blue & Gold Fleet Bay Cruise, Aquarium of the Bay, de Young Museum/Legion of Honor, the Exploratorium, San Francisco Museum of Modern Art, California Academy of Sciences & Steinhart Aquarium OR Asian Art Museum, and a seven-day all-access MUNI and Cable Car Passport (it costs $5 alone for a one-way ride on these historic and convenient gems!). Passes can be purchased online at www.citypass.com.

The **San Francisco Go Card**, a credit card-size discount pass, offers packages for 3, 5 or 7 day visits to many of the same attractions. Buy them at www.gosanfranciscocard.com.

Shopaholics should check out **Castro Street** not only for the historic theater, but for the offerings of its fun and quirky shops. Parents may want to shop elsewhere as many of the boutiques have an edgy and sometimes erotic bent; for details see Chapter 10, *Best Activities*.

Each June, the Gay and Lesbian community hosts one of the nation's largest **Pride Celebrations**. The parade alone draws nearly a half-million participants and spectators. **The Castor Street Fair** is another popular and creative fête held each October.

If you want to visit The Castro but aren't really sure how to navigate it alone, sign up for a City Guides' volunteer-led walking tour. **Castro: Tales of the Village** schleps you along the historic streets of this colorful district, from its humble beginnings as a working-class neighborhood anchored by immigrant homesteaders to its reputation as a rainbow-colored Gay Mecca. *Info*: The tour is offered year round most Sundays starting at 11am. Meet at the Harvey Milk Plaza at Castro and Market Streets under the large rainbow banner. www.sfcityguides.org.

Noe Valley

This shopper-friendly village is home to a cross-section of residents. Liberals and conservatives, as well as blue collar workers and those with six-figure incomes, live harmoniously in this

A Different Side of San Francisco

Consider one of these unusual tours to see a different side of the city:

• **Hobnob Tours** – A two-hour walking tour highlighting Nob Hill's ballrooms, mansions, cathedrals and scandals of high society. www.hobnobtours.com

• **Local Tastes of the City Tours** – Satisfy your cravings as you eat your way through the culinary history and culture of the city's local neighborhoods. www.sffoodtour.com

• **Mr. Treasure Hunt** – Play detective and solve clues as you learn about the hidden history and art of the city. www.mrtreasurehunt.com

• **Bay Quackers San Francisco Duck Tours** – Board an original, refurbished WWII amphibious landing craft for a 90-minute "surf & turf" tour of San Francisco's famous landmarks. www.bayquackers.com

• **Beat Walks** – Take a walking tour of North Beach and follow in the footsteps of The Beat and bohemian generations. www.beatwalks.com

• **Chinatown Adventure Tours with the "Wok Wiz"** – Join chef/author Shirley Fong-Torres as she traces Chinatown's history, folklore and, most importantly, food. www.wokwiz.com

• **Cruisin' the Castro Tours** – Learn the history and culture of one of the world's largest "Gay Meccas" on this fascinating rainbow walking tour. www.cruisinthecastro.com

• **The Gourmet Chocolate Tour** – Indulge on chocolate and walk it off at the same time on this delicious pedi-tour to some of the city's most renowned chocolatiers. www.gourmetwalks.com

• **Haight-Ashbury Flower Power Walking Tour** – Travel back in time to the Summer of Love on this 2-hour walking tour that revisits the free love, rock 'n' roll, and counter culture of the 1960s. www.haightashburytour.com

• **Javawalk** – Coffee lovers unite during this two-hour latte-style tour through the Old City. www.javawalk.com

• **San Francisco Movie Tours** – Go "on location" to visit the backdrops of movies set in San Francisco. Watch the actual film clips aboard a virtual "theater-on-wheels." www.sanfranciscomovietours.com

• **The Vampire Tour of San Francisco** – You've heard of the werewolves of London, now have a vis-à-vis with San Francisco's vampires…or at least learn how they have played an important role in the shaping of the city's gothic side. www.sfvampiretour.com

charming section of the city. The area doesn't offer much in the way of attractions or culture, but those who enjoy slipping into hip bistros, sleuthing the shelves of bookstores, or sipping espresso at the corner café will feel right at home in this non-touristy, yuppie kingdom where the stroller brigade is out in full force most every day of the week along bustling 24th Street.

For shopping details, see Chapter 10, *Best Activities*.

Named for the last Mexican mayor of Yerba Buena — present day San Francisco — this neighborhood boasts one of the highest concentrations of **row houses** within the city. But it's probably better known for its appearance in the Whoopi Goldberg film *Sister Act*, which featured the neighborhood's very own St. Paul's Catholic Church.

Saturday mornings are bustling at the **New Noe Valley Ministry** parking lot on 24th Street between Vicksburg and Sanchez. That's where the weekly **Farmers' Market** takes place from 8am until 12 noon rain or shine. Listen to live music, admire the organic fruits and veggies, or walk away with a bouquet of just-plucked pansies.

For a bit of a pick-me-up, scurry past the barista at Starbucks and, instead, head to **Lovejoy's English Tea Room**. Grab your best hen or bloke, hunker down on one of the couches, and treat yourself to scones topped with clotted cream, dainty sandwiches and, of course, a strong cuppa Afternoon Darjeeling. *Info*: 1195 Church Street.

Sausalito
Sausalito is a great day trip or half-day trip across the bay. The 30-

minute ferry ride is pleasant and quick. Catch the **Golden Gate Ferry** from the fabulous Ferry Building Marketplace at the foot of Market Street along the Embarcadero or the Blue and Gold Fleet near Pier 39 near Fisherman's Wharf. Once you arrive in town, stop by the Visitors' kiosk at the ferry boat landing for additional information.

This charming waterfront community has a European flair and is often compared to the French Riviera. The little willows — or *saucelitos* — growing along the shoreline prompted an 18th-century Spanish explorer to give the area its moniker. With less than 8,000 residents, many of them living in houseboats along the marina, the town is small and intimate.

Bridgeway is the main waterfront thoroughfare and is lined with shops, galleries and eateries (for shopping details, see Chapter 10, *Best Activities*). Here you can stroll at a leisurely pace, watch sea lions cavort near the water's edge, kick back in the town plaza or watch local residents practice their skills of balancing large rocks on top of one another along the shoreline. The **Bay Model Visitor Center**, a 1.5 acre working model of the bay, is located north of the village amid Sausalito's famed houseboat community. *Info*: Tel. 415/332-3871, 2100 Bridgeway.

You can also visit the **Bay Area Discovery Museum** and its interactive displays geared towards kids of all ages. For avid hikers and bikers, there are several well-groomed trails to venture on. *Info*: Tel. 415/339-3900, Fort Baker, 557 McReynolds Rd.

Take a tour of the **Heath Ceramics Factory** where skilled craftsmen have been producing award-winning tableware and architectural tiles since 1959. You'll witness the entire process, from clay making to kiln firing to the finished product, and might even find a piece or two to bring home. *Info*: www.heathceramics.com, Tel. 415/332-3732, 400 Gate Five Road.

When hunger strikes, I recommend two options. The first is to wander into **Venice Gourmet** across from the waterfront in the heart of town. This cramped shop doubles as a gourmet grocer and bona fide deli. Grab a couple of custom-made sandwiches (the Italian House Special is my favorite) and some bottles of sparkling water then head to a park bench overlooking the waterfront to enjoy an informal lunch while marveling at the spectacular views. *Info*: www.venicegourmet.com, Tel. 415/332-3544, 625 Bridgeway.

Another option, perhaps better suited for an evening meal, is **Angelino**, which is open for both lunch and dinner. Also located on the main drag, this intimate Italian bistro, with a mix of roomy booths and tables, specializes in southern Italian specialties. The wine list is a marriage of California and Italian vintages. Definitely order the house-baked focaccia bread sprinkled with rosemary and drizzled with olive oil. *Info*: www.angelinorestaurant.com, Tel. 415/331-5225, 521 Bridgeway.

Half Moon Bay
With an entire week to spend in San Francisco, set aside a day to venture to Half Moon Bay. Located less than 30 miles south of San Francisco, this sleepy outpost used to be a port of entry for rumrunners. Nowadays you're more likely to sip rum-infused drinks inside the swanky **Ritz-Carlton**, which is the only full-service resort in town. There are smaller inns, such as **Seal Cove Inn**, as well as a handful of quaint bed and breakfast hideaways (see Chapter 9, *Best Sleeps & Eats*).

For the most part, the beat of everyday life slows to a nice, leisurely pace within the city limits of this seaside community which rests at the base of the Santa Cruz Mountains. Spend time in the great outdoors doing a little tide pooling at **The Fitzgerald Marine Reserve**. A natural refuge for sea loving plants and animals whose habitats are close to the sea, a visit to the reserve may provide an opportunity to see everything from blue-green anemones to crabs and starfish up-close. During low tide, you can balance yourself atop normally submerged rocks and do some in-depth exploring along the ocean's surface.

If you happen to be in town during the winter or early spring, go whale watching aboard the *Salty Lady* with

Harbor Village

Check out **Harbor Village**, a new and much-needed addition to Half Moon Bay featuring a collection of 24 shops, restaurants and cafes set in a charming outdoor village. Designed as a turn-of-the century seaport, Harbor Village offers breathtaking views from every angle and a stunning all-glass octagonal shaped restaurant serving fresh seafood.

the **Oceanic Society**. The annual **gray whale migration** is touted as one of the most accessible wildlife spectacles as more than 15,000 mammals (the total population of the gray whale is only about 17,500) crowd the waters to swim south from the Arctic region to their breeding and calving grounds in the warm waters of Mexico. Each expedition features expert naturalists. Tours last about three hours and depart from Pillar Point Yacht Harbor. *Info*: www.oceanicsociety.com, Tel. 415/474-3385.

The town's historic **Main Street** features a collection of sidewalk cafes, boutiques and art galleries. The **San Benito House Deli** at 356 Main Street has fabulous sandwiches.

The beaches in Half Moon Bay—and most of Northern California—are chilly and wind swept. **Sea Horse Ranch & Friendly Acres Horse Rentals** will help you saddle up and enjoy a ride through coastal trails as well as on the pristine sands of the beach. *Info*: www.horserentals.com, Tel. 650/726-2362. Hiking and biking are also popular in these parts. You can easily rent a bike or use your two feet to explore **Half Moon Bay State Beach's Coastside Trail, McNee Ranch State Park** or the trail at **Gray Whale Cove State Beach**. You can also forge through the eucalyptus groves at **Burleigh Murray State Park**. Afterwards, reward yourself with a fabulous and well-earned spa treatment at the Ritz-Carlton.

As for nightlife, it's more sedate than the big city to the north, but it's not without a few after-dark offerings; see Chapter 10, *Best Activities*.

4. WINE COUNTRY: NAPA & SONOMA

A visit to California's **Wine Country** is an intoxicating experience. Located about an hour north of San Francisco — depending on the destination — the region is guilty of preying on every sense. There are verdant rolling hills and gangly grapevines stretched across the open land, coupled with gastronomical offerings and roadside tasting rooms destined for the epicurean traveler. While a car is needed to get around, the quaint villages are best experienced on foot. Spend time browsing through gourmet grocers, sleuthing for antiques and gifts (if not for someone back home, then definitely for yourself), tasting local vintages, and treating yourself to an escape behind the door of a local day spa.

Linking together **Napa Valley's** tuft of tiny towns is **Highway 29**, which connects the city of Napa with, from south to north, the villages of Yountville, Oakville, Rutherford, St. Helena and Calistoga. The **Silverado Trail**, which parallels Highway 29, is a lush and less commercial highway where many renowned wineries can be found.

Sonoma County is larger and much less continuous than Napa Valley. The county is about the size of Rhode Island with more than 80 miles of coastline along the Pacific Ocean and the San Pablo Bay. Sonoma is broken into three regions. The **Coasts and Sea Villages**, such as Bodega Bay and Timber Cove, reside on the fringes of the rugged Pacific Ocean. The **Rivers and Redwoods**, home to the Bohemian village of Guerneville, are scattered along the Russian River. The final region in this trifecta is the **Valleys and Vineyards**, which includes Sonoma, Santa Rosa and Healdsburg, features the resort communities with their town squares and upscale shops.

With all the edible offerings found in both Napa and Sonoma Counties — the cheese shops, fresh-pressed olive oil, just-plucked heirloom tomatoes, sweet sand dabs, and silky pinot noir — you can delightfully graze your way from town to town. Let's put it this way, if Tony Bennett left his heart in San Francisco chances are he left his palate in the Wine Country.

Did You Know ...?

- One barrel of wine yields about 20 cases or 1,200 glasses of vino.
- One ton of grapes is the equivalent of 720 bottles of wine or some 60 cases.
- A single vine can produce between four and six bottles of wine annually.
- A bottle of wine contains nearly 3 pounds of grapes, and each 5-ounce glass has more than a half-pound of the plump fruit as well.

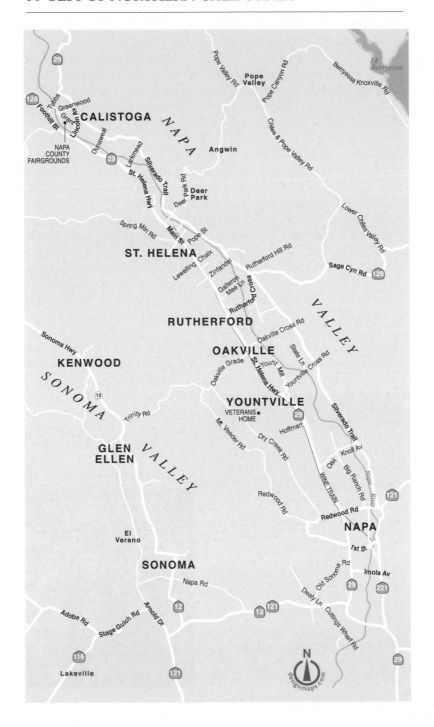

ONE GREAT DAY IN WINE COUNTRY

Begin the day at Sonoma's **Historic Plaza,** visit the historic **Mission San Francisco Solano,** spend a chunk of time at **Copia: The American Center for Wine, Food & the Arts,** have lunch at the **French Laundry** in Yountville, and do a little wine tasting along the way.

Make your way to Sonoma's Historic Plaza in the town of Sonoma for breakfast at **Sunflower Caffe** located on the plaza. Situated in an historic adobe that once belonged to Captain Vallejo, this local gathering spot is the perfect place for sipping strong espresso and noshing on oversized omelets. Try to snag a sidewalk table if possible. *Info*: 421 First Street West.

Afterwards, go window shopping on the square. Some not to be missed stores include **Wine Hardware,** everything for the enthusiast; **Chateau Sonoma,** a home and garden shop featuring treasures from the French countryside; and **Robin's Nest,** a gourmet kitchen store with gadgets galore. **Changing Seasons,** one of the many galleries on the plaza, features both local and international artists. Afterwards, see if you can sneak a peek inside the **Sebastiani Theatre.** This 1933 movie house, whose marquee still commands attention along the plaza, shows first-run films, as well as foreign flicks and film noir.

Next head to the site of the **Mission San Francisco Solano,** the 21st and final mission to be built and part of Sonoma State Historic Park. The mission, a white adobe

Did You Know ...?

Sonoma Plaza, designed some 150 years ago by Mexican Governor Mariano Vallejo and the largest of its kind in the state, is more than just a shopping and dining destination – it's a National Historic Landmark. The Plaza played a significant role in the shaping of California's history, including an event that was staged here in 1846 ending Mexico's control over California.

structure crowned by a red-tile roof, first celebrated mass on July 4, 1823. The mission system was established as a way to convert the native Indians into Christians by both the Catholic church and the Spanish government. It also helped to claim additional land for Spain. The church sold the mission in 1881 and it nearly met its demise two decades later. The only structure left is the long, low-slung building; the current chapel was built in 1841, but isn't considered part of the original structure. Inside are artifacts, lessons in constructing adobe homes, and more. *Info*: Tel. 707/938-1519. Sonoma Plaza, corner of Spain and 1st Streets.

ALTERNATIVE PLAN
If you're traveling with young children or if you just happen to be a railroad buff, head to nearby **Traintown** where you can ride the rails on a scale-model steam train. There's also a 47-foot clock tower and station modeled after Oakland, California's, 16th Street Depot and a trio of full-size cabooses hailing from the 1930s and '40s plus a petting zoo and amusement rides. *Info*: www.traintown.com. Tel. 707/938-3912. Sonoma, 20264 Broadway.

Next, head north on Highway 29 towards the town of **Napa**, home to **COPIA: The American Center for Food, Wine & the Arts**. This non-profit culinary center will appeal to gourmands and gardeners with its exceptional wine and food tasting programs, art exhibits, organic edible gardens, dining options, shopping and more. While exhibits and tastings change, a typical day at COPIA includes several scheduled lectures and tours, including complimentary wine tasting from the Winery of the Week, an orientation tour, introduction to wine tasting, wine and food pairings, garden tours, wine blending, and food classes. **Forks in the Road** is a permanent exhibition and COPIA's centerpiece that examines contemporary culture through shared expectations of food and drink that is both informative and interactive. Fans of the late Julia Child can admire her wall of copper pots, which actually adorned the iconic chef's very own kitchen.

There are also nearly 20 gardens, including the **COPIA Kids Garden** that encourages children of all ages to see, smell and touch the edibles. They can also visit with the many bunnies and chickens that call this patch of produce home. COPIA also offers special lecture series as well as an ongoing concert series where you can pick up a picnic dinner from **Julia's Kitchen**, the onsite restaurant named for America's favorite culinary innovator. *Info:*www.copia.org. Tel. 707/259-1600. Napa, 500 First Street.

After a few delicious hours at COPIA, continue north on Highway 29 stopping at a few select wineries. **Turnbull Wine Cellars** is known for their excellent selection of reds and one of the few wineries in Napa Valley that makes a syrah. *Info*: Turnbull offers tastings daily from 10am-4:30pm and tours are available by appointment only. www.turnbullwines.com. Tel. 800/887-6285 Ext. 18. Oakville, 8210 Highway 29.

Further north is **St. Supery Vineyards** in Rutherford, which offers both daily tastings and a discovery center to educate guests about wine and the winemaking process. *Info*: www.stsuppery.com. Tel. 707/963-4507. Rutherford, 8440 Highway 29. Still further, just past the town of St. Helena, is **St. Clements Vineyards** whose tasting room is housed in a hilltop Victorian manse that overlooks the entire valley. Known for their cabernets and chardonnays, this winery is one of Napa's most beautiful and offers picnic tables for lunching. *Info*: www.stclement.com. Tel. 800/331-8266. St. Helena, 2867 Highway 29.

Also located in St. Helena, just north of Downtown, is the **Culinary Institute of America's (CIA) West Coast campus**. Situated in and around the Greystone Cellars building, a stone structure erected in 1888 and listed on the **National Register of Historic Places,** the facility was owned by Christian Brothers who once produced sparkling wine on the premises. Now this magnificent structure is a learning center for those interested in the fields of food, wine, health and hospitality. Tours are offered on select days for just $5 per person, but you can prowl around a bit on your own inside the well-stocked culinary shop. The CIA is also home to the **Wine Spectator Greystone Restaurant**, where you can dine on the lovely terrace—weather permitting—or enjoy a drink by a roaring fire inside the lounge. *Info*: www.ciachef.edu. Tel. 707/967-1010. St. Helena, 2555 Main Street.

ALTERNATIVE PLAN

Not much of wine snob and don't care to be? How about treating your taste buds to some olive oil tastings? Wine may be Napa's main crop, but olives thrive in the warm, Mediterranean climate yielding plump fruit. Both **Long Meadow Ranch** in St. Helena (Tel. 707/963-4555) and **Round Pound** in Rutherford (Tel. 877/963-9364) offer guided walking olive mill tours and olive oil tastings. Tours are $35 at Long Meadow Ranch and $20 at Round Pound. Round Pound also offers **Al Fresco Lunches** (four person minimum) that includes both the olive mill tour and family-style lunch of artisan cheeses, meats, breads and other edibles, including an olive oil dessert cake. Tour reservations are required at both estates; call ahead.

Past St. Helena, at the very northern end of the Napa Valley, sits **Calistoga**. The town itself is quite charming and is known as California's spa town. Here you can soak in natural hot springs, wallow in thick gooey mud baths, and enjoy a relaxing massage at one of several spas. So have a signature soak at **Dr. Wilkinson's Hot Springs Resort**, an old-school style spa located on the main drag since 1946. For $169 you can get the works: mud bath with facial mask, aromatic mineral whirlpool bath, steam room, blanket wrap and a one-hour massage. *Info*: www.drwilkinson.com. Tel. 707/942-4102. Calistoga, 1507 Lincoln Avenue.

Or, if wallowing in mud sounds more primal than pampering, skip Doc Wilkinson's and head to **Old Faithful Geyser** instead – especially if you're traveling with children. This amazing geyser, one of only three Old Faithfuls in the entire world, is a natural phenomenon and a thrill to witness. Every 20-30 minutes Old Faithful erupts on cue, sending a searing surge of water as high as 75 feet into the air. In addition to the spectacle produced by Mother Nature, the grounds also feature Tennessee Fainting Goats, Jacob's Four-Horn Sheep, and Guard Llamas. *Info:*www.oldfaithfulgeyser.com. Tel. 707/942-6463. Calistoga, 1299 Tubbs Lane. Open daily from 9am-5pm – until 6pm in the summer. Admission: $8 adults, $3 children.

A FANTASTIC WINE COUNTRY WEEKEND

A weekend in the Wine Country can be the most romantic 72 hours of your life. It's a whirlwind of wine tasting, gourmet meals and village-style shopping. You'll want to visit some notable landmarks, soar above the vineyards in a **hot-air balloon**, enjoy a moveable feast from aboard the **Napa Wine Train**, and take a scenic drive to the coastal town of **Bodega Bay**, best known as the setting for Alfred Hitchcock's classic film *The Birds*.

Friday evening
Check into **Meadowood** in St. Helena (see *Best Sleeps & Eats* chapter) located on a winding road just off the Silverado Trail. Clusters of cottages cascade down the hillside, making this sprawling resort seem more like an elite country club. Each evening you can wander up to the reception area for a little complimentary wine and food pairing. After settling in, head to the resort's spa for a **Cabernet Crush** – a body treatment that includes a warm cabernet grape seed polish and a light brush massage. Then retreat to Meadowood's signature restaurant for a lavish meal or request room service and enjoy a romantic meal on your verandah with a bottle of wine before turning in for the night.

Saturday
Your day begins at sunrise aboard a hot-air balloon courtesy of **Bonaventura Ballooning**. You'll be ferried from the resort to the lift-off location courtesy of Bonaventura Ballooning. Upon arrival you can participate in the dramatic inflation or opt to be a curious spectator. Groups are intimate, usually 4-6 people per

gondola, and each trip is uniquely different as each journey's course is dictated by the weather and wind patterns. You'll drift above the vineyards and be rewarded at the end of your flight with a champagne toast and a sumptuous breakfast back at Meadowood. *Info*:www.bonaventuraballoons.com. Tel. 800/FLY-NAPA. $225 per person – breakfast included.

Once your feet are back on firm ground and you've had yourself a proper wine country breakfast, hop in the car for an afternoon drive. From **St. Helena**, you'll want to travel north on **Highway 128** passing through **Calistoga** and other small villages in order to make your way to **Highway 101** south. Once on Highway 101, you'll want to exit on **Highway 12** in Santa Rosa heading west through Sonoma County. Follow the road as you pass through Sebastopol and Bodega before the road ends at **Bodega Bay** and Highway 1 (note: Bodega and Bodega Bay are two separate towns, the former located a few miles inland the latter along the coast). Fans of Alfred Hitchcock's film, *The Birds*, may see a glimpse of familiar.

The town hasn't really changed all that much since Hollywood "discovered" it more than four decades ago. If you're into crabbing and fishing you may want to stop at **Doran County Park** and see

Fine Wine Country Dining

Looking for a great Wine Country meal? Check out these top Napa Valley restaurants and, to ensure you don't go hungry, make a reservation well in advance.

- **All Seasons Bistro** - Calistoga, Tel. 702/942-9111
- **La Toque** – Rutherford, Tel. 707/963-9770
- **Market** – St. Helena, Tel. 707/963-3779
- **The Restaurant at Meadowood** – St. Helena, Tel. 800/458-8080
- **Tra Vigne** – St. Helena, Tel. 707/963-4444
- **Ad Hoc** – Yountville, Tel. 707/944-2487
- **Mustards Grill** – Yountville, Tel. 707/944-2424

what you can catch from atop the jetties. There are birds in Bodega Bay, just not the murderous type conjured up in Hitchcock's psyche. A stroll around the headlands trail — allow at least an hour to complete the loop — will bring you beak-to-beak with the White-crowned and Savannah Sparrow. In fact, more rare birds have been spotted along Bodega Bay's headlands than in any other part of Sonoma County.

From Bodega Bay, head north up Highway 1 towards Jenner. It's a very scenic and leisurely drive as you pass by the headlands and the craggy coast. As you ramble along, take time to stop at one of the many parks or hike down to one of the beach's below. **Sonoma Coast State Beach**, which extends 17 miles from Bodega Head to Vista Trail just north of Jenner, is actually a series of beaches separated by rock bluffs and promontories. There are a dozen points along Highway 1 in which to access the beach. While you may have visions of wearing that new bikini, think again. The north coast weather is almost always foggy and even when it burns off, the cool ocean breezes will have you bundled up even during the summer. The shoreline is ideal

Hitchcock's Bodega Bay

Movie buffs can visit some of the locations used in the 1961 Alfred Hitchcock thriller *The Birds*. Those structures and locations that had starring roles include:

• The 150-year-old **Potter School**, which sits behind **St. Theresa's Church** in the town of Bodega (which you passed on your way into Bodega Bay). Today it is a private residence. The church is where the children took refuge from the flock of fowl.

• **Taylor Street** in Bodega Bay was where children could be seen running from the schoolhouse (even though the two are miles apart).

• The restaurant scenes, along with the gas station and boat dock, were filmed at **The Tides Restaurant** in Bodega Bay. The structure has since been rebuilt and is located across Highway 1 near the Visitors Center.

• The road where Tippi Hedren can be seen driving her Aston Martin into Bodego Bay were filmed on **Bay Hill Road**, about a mile north of the Visitors Center.

for beachcombing, fishing and picnicking – anything but sunbathing or swimming.

As you approach Jenner veer onto **Route116-Sonoma County Scenic Byway**. This road will lead you past acres of rolling vineyards, a number of bucolic towns, some tempting tasting rooms and the **Russian River** before it ends in **Sebastopol**. Along the way you'll find there is never a shortage of wine tasting and vineyard tour opportunities as you meander past the hamlets belonging to the **Rivers and Redwoods** region: Jenner, Duncan Mills, Monte Rio, and Guerneville.

ALTERNATIVE PLAN
Best enjoyed during the summer months, the banks along the **Russian River** are a great escape for fishing and swimming. River access is available at many points along the shoreline. The Russian River region lends itself well to bikini-clad visitors from May to October. You may want to head to **Johnson's Beach** in downtown Guerneville, which is an ideal place to launch a canoe, kayak or paddleboat. Plus the parking is free.

One stop I highly recommend is to the **Korbel Champagne Cellars** located just outside the town of **Guerneville**. The 50-minute **Champagne Cellars Tour**, which depart every 45 minutes daily from 10am to 3pm and are free to the public, takes you through the antique vaults where the first bottles of bubbly were made more than a century ago. You'll also learn the history of Korbel, how the family stumbled upon wine making, and how champagne is made. Afterwards, you'll retreat with your tour guide and fellow tour goers to participate in a champagne tasting, including a sip of the champagne poured at the presidential inauguration. In fact, Korbel has been the exclusive champagne for the past five presidential inaugurations and was the champagne of choice inside the White House during the Kennedy Camelot years. There is also a beautiful rose garden opened for tours, as well as a delicatessen and market serving gourmet grub and wines by the glass that are best enjoyed on the outdoor patio beneath the aged redwood trees. *Info:*www.korbel.com. Tel. 707/ 824-7000. Guerneville. 13250 River Road.

As you approach Sebastopol, you may want to stop to browse through the antique shops in the historic downtown area. If you're hungry, stop into **Starlight Wine Bar and Restaurant** for a full meal or the charcuterie plate paired with local wines. The restaurant, housed in a vintage **Pullman Streamliner** train car, allows you to create your own wine flights. If you've had your fill of wine tasting, you can enjoy one of several beers on tap. *Info:* www.starlightwinebar.com. 707/823-1943. Sebastopol, 6761 Sebastopol Avenue.

The Santa Express

If you visit in mid-to-late December, have the kids join you aboard the Napa Valley Wine Train's **Santa Express**. The train travels from Napa to Yountville and includes such VIP passengers as Santa, his elves and some cheery carolers. There are also photo opportunities with St. Nick. Rates start at $25 per person, and kids under 12 ride free with each paying adult. Food and beverage not included, but available for purchase onboard. *Info:* Tel. 800/427-4124.

Sunday

You'll want to eat a light this morning and maybe spend some time out by the pool before you motor to Napa to board the **Napa Valley Wine Train**. Critics have been harsh since its inaugural ride back in the early 1990s. Many claim the food to be so-so and the cost too expensive, but the

Napa Valley Wine Train, like so many other signature attractions in other parts of the world, is one of those must-try-once experiences.

Check in is at 11:30 a.m. for the **Domaine Chandon Sparkling Winery Tour & Gourmet Lunch** and a pre-boarding wine tasting gets underway shortly after arrival. Once onboard the vintage Pullman Railcar, you'll sit back and enjoy the ride on a moving piece of history which travels on a rail line built in 1847. The fleet of railcars have been restored to their original elegance and each boasts four parlor cars, four dining cars, and a kitchen car. Your moveable feast includes a gourmet lunch on board, a private tour and tasting at Domaine Chandon Winery, afternoon tea and shopping. *Info:*www.winetrain.com. Tel. 800/427-4124. Napa. 1275 McKinstry Street. $89 per person.

A WONDERFUL WEEK IN THE WINE COUNTRY

After a week in the Wine Country, you'll have come to know the region and its vintages quite well. You'll return home a bit of an oenophile having had a chance to explore and visit the many tasting rooms that dot the countryside. Chances are you'll have explored some of the region's charming town squares, visited some unique attractions and, given the opportunity, draped yourself across a massage table for some much-needed kneading. From the rugged coast to the dense redwoods, hiking or biking, you'll be amazed at how refreshed you feel upon check out.

RECOMMENDED PLAN: You'll want to incorporate many of the suggestions in the *One Great Day* and *A Fantastic Weekend* sections detailed on the previous pages: **The Napa Wine Train**, a hot-air balloon ride, a visit to **Old Faithful Geyser**, and an afternoon spent at **COPIA**. You'll also want to explore some of the area's charming town squares, including Sonoma and Healdsburg, visit the ruins of **Jack London's** dream house in Glen Ellen, trek through the

Petrified Forest in Calistoga, take a scenic drive along the coast and, without a doubt, visit some noted wineries. A week in this boozy bucolic region with also leave you with plenty of time to take a day trip elsewhere. I suggest you temporarily cork the bottle of cabernet and, instead, take a sojourn to **San Francisco**, located about an hour's drive from Napa (see Chapter 3 for details).

If you're staying an entire week in the Wine Country, you can divide your time by staying in two locales. I first recommend checking into **MacArthur's Place** in the town of Sonoma or the **Kenwood Inn & Spa** in nearby Kenwood; then spend the latter half of your week at a Napa resort, perhaps **Meadowood Resort** in St. Helena or **Cottage Grove Inn** near downtown Calistoga. Check out these and other Wine Country recommendations in the *Best Sleeps & Eats* chapter.

The best way to explore the Wine Country is via car, either you appoint yourself as designated driver or hire one of the many limousine-cum-wine tour companies to ferry you around. Small hamlets are laced together by Route 12 in Sonoma and Route 29 in Napa, and it's best to steer clear of these byways during commuter congestion – generally weekdays from 7am-9am and 4pm-6pm. There are also a number of rambling roads that re-  quire a more leisurely pace and yield some spectacular scenery.

Don't simply drive through the Wine Country, make time to stop and smell the grapes and explore the region's charming towns.

Sonoma County

Both **Sonoma** and **Healdsburg** have historic town plazas filled with shops, acclaimed restaurants, galleries and other amenities. During the summer residents spill out into the grassy center squares to prowl for heirloom tomatoes at the **weekly farmers' market** or stake claim to a park bench to enjoy a **free concert** under the stars. Accompanying the strains of jazz and blues are the sounds of corks being unleashed from wine bottles produced by local vintners.

In Sonoma, check out these key historic sites along Sonoma Plaza:
* **Salvador Vallejo Home** at 415 First St. W. – built by General Vallejo's brother in the early 1840s.
* **Swiss Hotel** at 18 W. Spain Street – also built by Salvador Vallejo in the late 1830s as his residence and converted to a hotel in the late 19th century.
* **Casa Grande**, situated between the Swiss and Toscano Hotels on Spain Street – the site of the first adobe home of General Vallejo and built in 1836 while Sonoma was a Mexican pueblo.
* **Toscano Hotel** at 20 E. Spain Street – opened in the 1850s as a general store and library before its conversion to a hotel in 1886.
* **Sonoma Barracks** at Spain and 1st Streets – constructed in 1836 by General Vallejo.
* **Bear Flag Monument on the Plaza** – where an American horseman rode into Sonoma on June 14, 1846, proclaiming the "California Republic" as he raised the original Bear Flag.
* **Mission San Francisco Solano de Sonoma** at Spain and 1st Streets – erected in 1823 and the last of the 21 California missions to be built.

About a five minute drive from Sonoma is one of my favorite wineries, **Buena Vista Winery**. Founded in 1857, Buena Vista is the state's oldest premium winery with California Historic Landmark status. The tasting room, housed in a stunning stone building, welcomes oenophiles daily from 10am-5pm. Stop by **Sonoma Market** to order your picnic edibles. *Info*: www.sonoma-glenellenmkt.com. Tel. 707/996-3411. 500 W. Napa Street. They have a sister market in Glen Ellen, too, called the Glen Ellen

Pace Yourself at the Wineries!

The key to wine tasting is knowing how to pace yourself and finding a winery that caters to your specific needs.

• Rutherford's **Cakebread Cellars** is for aspiring vintners who are thirsty to learn all about the winemaking process. *Info*: www.cakebread.com. Tel. 800/588-0298.

• Television junkies may enjoy a stop to **Spring Mountain Vineyards** in St. Helena, known for its superb Cabernets Sauvignons and as the setting for *Falcon's Crest*. *Info*: www.springmtn.com. Tel. 707/967-4188.

• For intoxicating views and extended wine tasting hours, make Napa's **Domaine Carneros** your last stop for a swill. *Info*: www.domaine.com. Tel. 800 716-BRUT (2788).

• Grab a picnic hamper from nearby **Oakville Grocers** and have yourself a feast at **Rutherford Hill Winery** in Rutherford. Purchase a bottle of their merlot to enjoy with your lunch. *Info*: www.rutherfordhill.com. Tel. 707/963-1871.

• Why does St. Helena's **V. Sattui Winery** (*photo below*) have such long queues? The tastings are free, a rare find in Napa Valley. You can purchase a bottle, grab some cheese and crackers from the deli, and enjoy a picnic near the fountain. *Info*: www.vsattui.com. Tel. 707/963-7774.

• Belly up to the bar along Napa's Silverado Trail at **Robert Sinskey Vineyards**, which feels more like a wine bar than a tasting room. A gluttonous flight will cost you $20, but $15 is refundable if you purchase two or more bottles of vino. *Info*: www.robertsinskey.com. Tel. 707/944-9090.

Village Market. Pick up a premium bottle of wine at Buena Vista and enjoy a lovely wine country lunch on the grounds. *Info*: www.buenavistacarneros.com. Tel. 800/926-1266. 18000 Old Winery Road.

Glen Ellen is yet another small hamlet with its modest share of inns, restaurants and wineries. San Francisco native and writer Jack London lived in Sonoma from 1909 until his death in 1916 building his Beauty Ranch and manse, the Wolf House, which burned to the ground on the eve his wife Charmian and he were to move in. The ruins of Wolf House is now part of **Jack London State Historic Park**. This nearly 900-acre wooded sanctuary features hiking trails, the graves of Jack and Charmian London, and several ranch buildings. The **House of Happy Walls**, built after London's death by his wife, is a museum containing an extensive library, original furnishings, and memorabilia, such as the couple's collection of finds from the South Pacific. *Info*:www.parks.sonoma.net. Tel. 707/938-5216. 2400 London Ranch Road. Open daily from 10am-5pm. $6 per car.

While in Glen Ellen, make a point to visit the **Imagery Estate Winery & Art Gallery**, where a majority of the wines offered can only be purchased on the premises. The tasting room is inviting, and you're welcome to enjoy a glass on the umbrella-laden patio. The wines are also labeled with original artwork, and the onsite gallery houses the world's largest wine label art collection with commissioned pieces by such notable talents as Sol Lewitt, William Wiley and Judy Pfaff. *Info*: www.imagerywinery.com. Tel. 707/835-4515. 14335 Highway 12.

Petaluma, the hometown of actress Winona Ryder, is more working class than tourist driven. A true Victorian riverfront town, the downtown area features a collection of shops, selection of nice dining options, antique stores, and more. The **Great Petaluma Mill** is a collection of four riverfront buildings, including an 1854 warehouse reported to be the town's oldest, filled with shops, espresso bars and a fitness center. The town is also a favorite of location scouts who enjoy casting Petaluma as the backdrop in feature films. Scenes from the classic film *American Graffiti* were filmed on the town's main street, as were *Basic*

Instinct and *Peggy Sue Got Married*. *The Horse Whisperer*, starring Robert Redford, was also filmed in Petaluma.

Can't bear to cross the threshold of yet another tasting room? Then consider visiting one of these unique non-vintner Sonoma venues:

- Tour America's Favorite Sticker Factory at **Mrs. Grossman's Paper Company** in Petaluma, the only sticker company in the country with its own printing plant on-site. *Info:* www.mrsgrossmans.com. Tel. 800/429-4549.
- Visit the **Charles M. Schultz Museum & Research Center** in Santa Rosa to see the drawings, awards, photographs and memorabilia of the creator of the *Peanuts* comic strip. *Info:* www.charlesmshultzmuseum.org. Tel. 707/579-4452.
- Take a cooking class at **Ramekins** in Sonoma where visiting chefs teach soup to nuts courses. *Info:* www.ramekins.com. Tel. 707/933-0450.
- Enjoy a film noir at the historic **Sebastiani Theatre** overlooking Sonoma Plaza. Built in 1933, this classic movie house also hosts special events and entertainers. *Info:* www.sebastianitheatre.com. Tel. 707/996-9756.
- Discover some animal magnetism at **Safari West Wildlife Preserve & Resort** in Calistoga where more than 400 mammals and birds roam and flutter. *Info:* www.safariwest.com. Tel. 707/579-2551.

Santa Rosa

Santa Rosa is the largest city in Sonoma County, but it has managed to retain its charm and small town feel nonetheless. **Downtown Santa Rosa** is quite enchanting and a good place to spend an afternoon. Visit the historic **Railroad Square** where new and restored vintage buildings house antique shops and fine restaurants. *Info:* www.railroadsquare.com. Tel. 707/578-8478. Corner of 4th & Wilson Streets

Nearby is **Courthouse Square**, a pedestrian-friendly shopping area fraught with more shops, restaurants and the **Sonoma County Museum**, which is housed in a former 1910 post office boasting a collection of art, history and cultural exhibitions. The

Russian River's Top 10

Take a **scenic drive** through the rivers and redwoods in Sonoma's **Russian River region** and try some of the following:

• A meal at **River's End** where the Russian River and Pacific Ocean collide just north of Bodega. *Info:* www.ilovesunsets.com. Tel. 707/865-2484.
• Sipping a sample of presidential inaugural champagne at the **Korbel Champagne Cellars**. *Info:* www.korbel.com. Tel. 707/824-7000.
• Pitching a tent and setting up camp at one of the many riverfront campgrounds.
• Taking a lazy canoe or kayak trek down the Russian River.
• Collecting seashells along the rugged and cragged coastline.
• Picnicking in the shadow of an **aged redwood** on a sunny afternoon.
• Plunging into the deep, cool waters of **Lake Sonoma**.
• Treating yourself to a crushed grape body treatment at some posh spa.
• Eating plump, juicy grapes straight from the vine.

area in and around Courthouse Square is laden with fountains and features a classic park setting. *Info:* www.sonomacountymusuem.com. Tel. 707/579-1500. 425 Seventh Street. $5 adults, $3 children.

In the vicinity is the **Luther Burbank Home and Gardens** where the famed horticulturist lived while developing new strains of plants and improving the world's food supply. During his many years in Santa Rosa, he introduced some 200 varieties of fruits, vegetables, grains and ornamental flowers, most notably the Burbank Russet Potato, the Shasta Daisy and the Santa Rosa Plum. *Info:* www.parks.sonoma.net/burbank.html. Tel. 707/524-5445. Santa Rose and Sonoma Avenues.

If you have kids in tow and want to just enjoy a simple day outdoors, make Santa Rosa's **Howarth Park** part of your agenda. The 152-acre greenbelt offers such simple pleasures as a train ride, carousel, and pony rides. You can rent paddle boats, kayaks, row boats and sail boats at the park's boat house near the lake. There is also fishing, climbing walls, and picnic areas worthy of your time. *Info*: http://ci.santa-rosa.ca.us. Tel. 707/543-3282. 415 Steele Lane.

5. THE CENTRAL COAST: SANTA CRUZ TO CAMBRIA

Few places can rival the beauty of California's Central Coast. Its wild and wondrous shoreline is full of pleasures. Jagged cliffs, photogenic scenery and long stretches of isolation create a sculpted work of art. The region, which stretches **north of Santa Barbara proper to Santa Cruz,** quickly puts you in relaxation mode with its slower, more enjoyable pace. The expanse of coastline, unforgettable sights, and breathtaking scenery gives California bragging rights to having one of the nation's most beautiful provinces. The small to mid-size coastal towns that punctuate the Central Coast pack a punch with their historical offerings, not-to-miss attractions, and natural wonders.

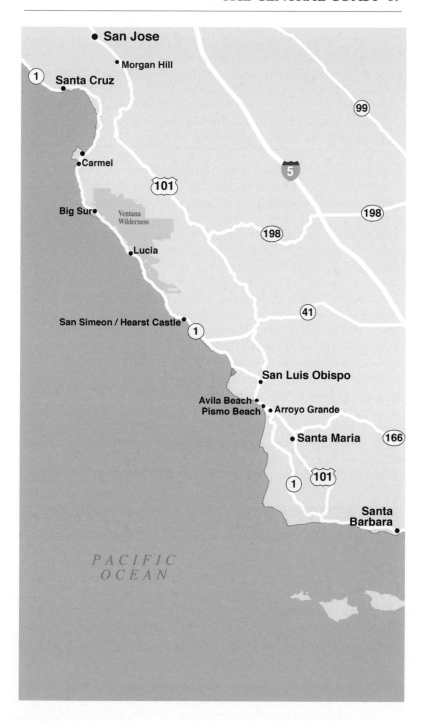

Cambria, located at the southern tip of the region, is a small hamlet located a few miles from Hearst Castle. Much further up the coast is **Big Sur**, a flower power layover (though some never left) during the hippie exodus to San Francisco in the late '60s, known for its pristine coastline, unspoiled beauty, and pair of celebrity-favored hideaways. **Monterey** is a great destination for families with its Cannery Row and renowned aquarium.

Neighboring Monterey is the vanguard village of **Carmel** with its Hansel and Gretel-like architecture, vacationing celebrities, and home to world-class golfing at neighboring **Pebble Beach**. **Santa Cruz**, a laidback surf ghetto and home to the University of California, Santa Cruz, where the Banana Slug is the school mascot), features an old-fashioned, seaside boardwalk lined with amusements and rides.

The Central Coast, with the exception of Santa Cruz, has all the trappings needed for a Zen-like holiday. The sound of chirping birds and pounding waves replaces city noise, while multi-lane freeways give way to leisurely lanes that offer stomach-churning twists and turns high above the ocean bluffs. Like much of Northern California, there's opportunity to do a little wine tasting, slip behind the doors of some spa sanctuary for some much-needed body therapy, prowl through art galleries and boutiques, and embrace the great outdoors with a hike through the wilderness. After spending substantial time along the Central Coast, chances are you'll quickly adapt to the snail's pace way of living. What more could you ask for?

ONE GREAT DAY ALONG MONTEREY BAY

It's impossible to do the entire Central Coast in one day, unless you consider being behind the wheel of your car an exciting prospect. So, for practical purposes, we'll focus on enjoying the riches of **Carmel, Monterey** and **Pacific Grove**, towns of varying size clustered closely together.

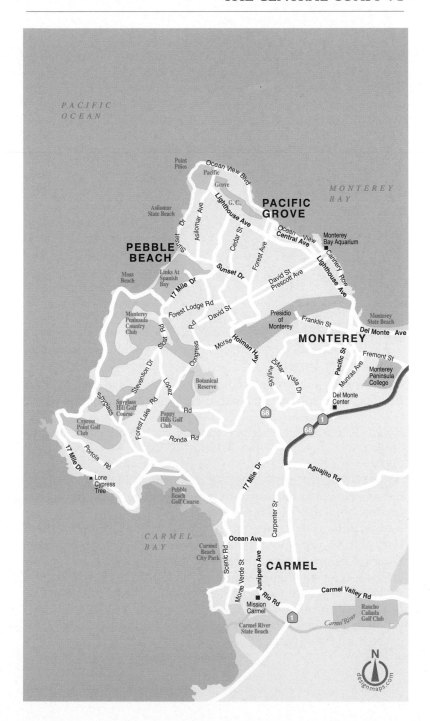

Begin the day in the quaint town of Carmel-by-the-Sea, which everyone shortens to Carmel, with breakfast at **The Cottage Restaurant** (with a name like that, how can you go wrong?). Graze on an assortment of egg dishes, feather-light crepes, and other morning fare before visiting the cloistered **Mission Carmel**, whose formal name is **San Carlos Borroméo del Rio Carmelo**.

Every fourth grade student attending the state's public schools is taught the history of the mission system founded by Father Junipero Serra and, you too, can get a crash course in California history just by spending a couple of hours on the premises. This mission, the second in the 21 fleet, was founded in 1771 and served as the headquarters for the entire mission system under Father Serra. Take a self-guided or docent-led tour at this active and sequestered parish. *Info*: www.carmelmission.org. Tel. 831/624-3600. Carmel, 3080 Rio Road. Tours are just $5 per person, and available Monday-Saturday from 9:30am-5pm; Sunday 10:30am-5pm.

After visiting the mission, make it your mission to stroll along Ocean Avenue in the heart of Carmel's village. Here you'll find quaint shops tucked inside even quainter buildings, many that look as if they were ripped from the pages of a Grimm Brothers fairy tale. An assembly of pine trees adorns the center medium of **Ocean Avenue**, which terminates near the sand. Take time to stroll the crescent-shaped shoreline, which can be cold during the months you would typically be sweating. On your way to the beach, venture off the beaten path to wander through the residential neighborhood. There are no sidewalks, but that's okay because traffic is minimal at best.

Charming Carmel

Part of Carmel's charm, besides its darling Comstock-style cottages, is that **there are no street addresses** assigned to homes. Although mail carriers and the FedEx guy might not find it so endearing, this is how its residents like it. Properties are identified by their location, for example, here's one pulled from the city's website: located at the "west side of San Antonio three houses south of 12th Avenue." Homes are also located by names, such as the "Tinker Bell" cottage.

Next, gas up for an excursion along **17-Mile Drive**, perhaps one of California's most scenic routes, and be sure your camera has either plenty of film or enough memory to capture its beauty. There is an entrance fee of $9, which is collected at any one of Pebble Beach Resorts five gates; motorcycles are not permitted. The drive, which has 21 optional stops, was originally created by the old Del Monte Hotel as a way to lure guests to the property by offering them a delightful carriage ride to what was then the rustic Lodge at Pebble Beach. I think you'll agree that it's rustic no longer.

You'll begin your journey in Carmel and, once the loop is complete, you'll end here as well. Along the way discover a treasure trove of wonders left by Mother Nature: the canopied **Del Monte Forest**; the 250-year-old **Lone Cypress**, perched on a barren precipice high above the ocean (*see photo at right*); **Bird Rock** where countless fowl and sea lions gather; and **Crocker Grove**, a 13-acre nature sanctuary. Man has left his indelible mark here as well in the form of emerald green golf courses and five-star luxury hideaways. Stop along the way to have lunch at

Stillwater Bar & Grill overlooking the fairway at the Lodge at Pebble Beach. Compared to the resorts' other restaurants, it's a bit lighter on your wallet. If you're not staying at one of the Pebble Beach Resorts, you may want to stroll around one of the hotels, such as **The Lodge at Pebble Beach** or the **Inn at Spanish Bay** – both of which always receive rave reviews from the media. In addition to the natural wonders and five-star resorts, 17-mile Drive also has some unbelievable estates to ogle at as you casually motor by.

ALTERNATIVE PLAN
Either **purchase a picnic lunch** before you begin 17-Mile-Drive at a local grocery store or stop at the **Pebble Beach Market** en route and grab a prepared basket lunch to enjoy somewhere along the way at a designated picnic area.

After you've finished 17-Mile-Drive, it's onto the **Monterey Bay Aquarium.** Opened in 1984, the aquarium was built on the site of the old Hovden Cannery along Cannery Row. The cannery, closed since 1973, was last operated by Portola Packing Company before it was purchased by Stanford University who then sold it to the Monterey Bay Aquarium Foundation. Construction began on the aquarium in 1980; today there are nearly 200 galleries and exhibits devoted entirely to the habitats of the local waters. Among the four largest exhibits are the Outer Bay; the Kelp Forest; Monterey Bay Habitats; and Sea Otters that frolic along the Rocky Coast. The aquarium is also home to the world's largest jelly fish galleries. There are also several feeding demonstrations throughout the day where sea otters and penguins can be seen grazing, as well as a kelp forest dive show. There is even a walk-through aviary and an indoor play area for younger visitors. The aquarium is a

great stop for marine enthusiasts and even a better stop for families. If you want to picnic on-site, there is an area located behind the Education Building or you can picnic along the outside amphitheatre at the Great Tide Pool. The aquarium also houses a full-service restaurant.

You may want to visit the Aquarium's website and click on "Visitor Info" to see which hotels are participating in a complete package, including accommodations and two adult tickets to the aquarium. You can also save money if you are an active or retired member of the military or if you belong to a credit union that has partnered with the aquarium. *Info*: www.montereybayaquarium.org. Tel. 800/756-3737. 886 Cannery Row. Open daily 10am-6pm. Adults $24.95, children $15.95.

After the aquarium, which could take a few hours or several hours, depending on your fetish for fish, walk along **Cannery Row** and then over to **Pacific Grove** – which is literally a few steps from the aquarium. The shoreline is really beautiful, and the town is flanked with stunning Victorian homes. If you happen to be in the area from October through early March, you'll want to visit the **Monarch Butterfly Sanctuary** governed by the **Pacific Grove Museum of Natural History**. During these wintry months, groups of monarch butterflies can be seen clustered together in thick bunches on pine and eucalyptus trees, which has earned Pacific Grove the nickname "Butterfly Town, U.S.A." On the second Saturday of October the town is aflutter as the Pacific Grove School District holds its annual Butterfly Parade. Local children and their teachers dress in costume and sashay through town to celebrate the return of these colorful creatures.

Should you be visiting in the spring and summer when the butterflies aren't present, take a tour of **Point Pinos Lighthouse**. This is the third lighthouse established in California—after Alcatraz and Fort Point—and is located on the northernmost tip of the peninsula. Its beacon has guided sailors since February 1, 1855, shortly after California became a state. The building, lenses and prisms of the light are all original, and Point Pinos is the oldest continuously operating lighthouse on the West Coast. Listed on the National Register of Historic Places, the lighthouse was finally automated in 1975. It's now open to the public Thursday-Monday from 10am-4pm for tours. *Info*: To visit either the Monarch Butterfly Sanctuary or the Point Pinos Lighthouse, stop into the Pacific Grover Natural History Museum. www.pgmuseum.org. Tel. 831/648-5716. 165 Forest Avenue. They can provide directions and additional information. Open Tuesday-Sunday 10am-5pm.

ALTERNATIVE PLAN
Sierra Mar is an ideal restaurant for adults, but it's completely inappropriate for kids. If you're traveling with children, stay put in Pacific Grove and head to **Fish Wife**. Not only are kids welcomed, their menu is the same as their adult counterparts only served in age-appropriate portions. See the *Best Sleeps & Eats* chapter for more information.

As the day winds down, hop in the car and head towards **Big Sur** before sunset. You'll dine at **Sierra Mar** at **Post Ranch Inn** overlooking the Pacific Ocean and boasting million-dollar views. Guests not staying at the hotel are seated for dinner at 5:30pm, 6pm or 8:30pm. Be sure to make a reservation ahead of time, and shoot for one of the earlier seatings so you can view the sun setting. As you savor your four-course meal and wine (the wine list, by the way, is more of a tome than a list), you'll simply be overwhelmed by the views.

A FANTASTIC CENTRAL COAST WEEKEND

Even though you'll be bouncing around the **Monterey Peninsula** and **Big Sur**, this will be a busy but relaxing weekend. You'll do a little wine tasting, sleuth through art galleries and shops, stroll along the waterfront admiring nature just off shore, and do a little hiking, too. You'll also visit the **National Steinbeck Center** to experience a journey through the words of John Steinbeck, the Central Coast's favorite son. At night, you can stargaze, head to a pub to hang with the locals or read Steinbeck's *Cannery Row* while lounging in your hotel room.

Friday Night
Arrive in time to enjoy drinks and appetizers at **Cielo**, part of
Ventana Inn and Spa in Big Sur. You don't have to be a guest to
avail yourself to the outdoor lounge — complete with fire pit,
unbelievable views, and a wine list that is as long as it is varied.
The lounge is open from 3:30-5:30pm. If you're traveling as a
twosome, this is a very romantic destination for a stolen weekend; however, if you're traveling with kids I recommend the
Cypress Inn in downtown Carmel, which also accommodates
pets. See the *Best Sleeps & Eats* chapter for more information.

Assuming you're traveling with no kids and have chosen to stay
at the Ventana Inn and Spa, book the **Couples Experience Massage** for later that evening. The two of you will enjoy a rubdown
side-by-side either in your room or in the Couple's Suite at the
spa. Included are a relaxing bath by candlelight, music of your
choice, chocolate truffles, and tea. At $485 for 100 minutes of
mind blowing relaxation, it doesn't come cheap but it's a wonderful way to begin your weekend.

Saturday
Grab breakfast, and then head to the **National Steinbeck Center**
in **Salinas**. The museum explores the life and works of writer
John Steinbeck, whose boyhood home is a few steps from the
center. The Central Coast was the inspiration for many of his
stories, and his words have been brought to life through interactive exhibits, films and events. Visitors can access Steinbeck's
works on CD-ROM or explore their own creativity in the "Art of
Writing" room. The changing exhibit gallery also accommodates
a variety of art and cultural presentations. If you're visiting the
area in early August, plan on attending the annual **Steinbeck
Festival**, a multi-day happening that includes lectures, exhibits,
and a street fair all celebrating the life and times of John Steinbeck.
Info: www.steinbeck.org. Tel. 831/796-3833. Salinas, One Main
Street. Open daily 10am-5pm. Adults $10.95, children $7.95.

Work up an appetite wandering through the National Steinbeck
Center, then head to the birthplace and childhood home of **John
Steinbeck** just two blocks away. This lovely Queen Anne Victo-
rian treasure is where the author took his first breath on February

27, 1902 (the house was built in 1897 and the Steinbeck family settled down here in 1900). **The Steinbeck House**, which displays photos and memorabilia, is open Monday-Saturday for lunch 11:30am-2pm. The restaurant has a menu that changes weekly and features locally-grown produce plus Monterey County beer and wines. On occasion there is also a full-service afternoon tea. *Info*: www.steinbeckhouse.com. Tel. 831/424-2735. Salinas. 132 Central Avenue.

Plan on spending the afternoon doing some **wine tasting** at the various vintners scattered across Monterey County. Most people quickly associate California wine producers with those in Napa and Sonoma, but Monterey County actually sells their grapes to other vintners throughout the state. There are some 40,000 acres devoted entirely to producing wine grapes, and there are several wineries that open their doors for both tastings and tours. From Salinas, take Main Street (Highway 68) to Laureles Grade Road and make a left. Follow the road for about six miles and turn left on Carmel Valley Road. Along **Carmel Valley Road** you'll find signs leading to several wineries, including **Heller Estate, Talbott, Bernardus, Joullian, Chateau Sinnet**, and **San Saba**. Afterwards, you can head to back on Carmel Valley Road to Highway 1. Take Highway 1 and follow the signs

Steinbeck Gift Shop

Located in the basement of **The Steinbeck House** restaurant is **The Best Cellar**, a delightful gift shop offering a collection of unique gift items coupled with vintage and newly printed Steinbeck books. There is also original furniture from the Steinbeck family on display, including the headboard taken from the bed in which the author was born.

leading to **Cannery Row** in Monterey where you can do more wine tasting in town at **A Taste of Monterey, Clos LaChance, Silver Mountain,** and **Baywood Cellars,** which are all clustered together. Most wineries in Monterey County charge a modest tasting fee; however, fees are typically waived if you purchase a bottle of wine.

ALTERNATIVE PLAN

If this is a family trip and the kids are along, say so long to the syrah and instead visit **Wild Things** in Salinas. Located on Vision Quest Ranch, the facility provides wild and exotic birds and animals to the film industry. The sanctuary is open daily for tours, which include a video presentation and a look at the inventory of animal actors, from cats to bears to elephants. Tours are offered at 1pm only; at 1pm and 3pm during summer months. *Info:* www.wildthingsinc.com. Tel. 831/ 455-1901. Salinas, 400 River Road. Adults $10, children $8.

If you still have time, explore more of **Cannery Row** and **Downtown,** which are separated from one another by the Presidio. **Cannery Row,** as chronicled in John Steinbeck's novel of the same name, was a thriving area during the 1920s and '30s. A fleet of sardine canneries lined the waterfront creating a bustling industry for the town. Some of the buildings remain, but the silvery fish have since been replaced by colorful shops, restaurants and galleries. Downtown Monterey or, as it's often referred to, Old Monterey, features a collection of historic buildings and a lively, if not touristy, **Old Fisherman's Wharf,** established in 1845, with more shops and restaurants, seasonal whale watching excursions, and kayak rentals.

Downtown shops and restaurants are found along its main thoroughfare, **Alvarado Street,** as well as neighboring streets. Every Tuesday this area stages one of the state's largest farmers' markets. Not surprising: nearby Castroville is touted as the "Artichoke Capital of the World." Its annual festival, which pays tribute to the layered vegetable, dates back to the 1940s. The very first **Artichoke Queen** was a young Hollywood starlet named Norma Jean Baker, who was later transformed into a blonde bombshell known to the world as **Marilyn Monroe.**

Monterey's Top 10

- Pet sharks and other underwater creatures at the hands-on touch pools at the **Monterey Bay Aquarium.**
- Be inspired at the **National Steinbeck Center** in Salinas.
- See seals, otters, and other marine life at Seal Rock Picnic Area along **17-Mile Drive.**
- Experience the **migration of Monarch butterflies**, October to March, in Pacific Grove.
- Tour one of California's oldest seafaring beacons, **Point Pinos Lighthouse.**
- Take a **stroll through history** on a walking tour of Monterey's 40-plus adobes and historic buildings.
- Get wild with lions, tigers, birds and reptiles used for movie and television shoots at **Wild Things** in Salinas.
- Hike to the cove that inspired Robert Louis Stevenson's novel *Treasure Island* at **Point Lobos State Reserve.**
- Explore **Cannery Row** and **Fisherman's Wharf.**
- Bellow "thar she blows" after spotting a mighty mammal on a **whale watching tour.**

Spend the rest of your evening in Carmel with a sunset walk along the beach. Then stroll up to **Bouchée Restaurant & Wine Bar** on Mission Street between Ocean and Seventh, to sample steamed mussels and fois gras paired with local vintages. If you're staying at the Cypress Inn, their intimate bar is a delightful place for a nightcap.

Sunday

Wake up early and enjoy a leisurely breakfast at your hotel. You've spent most of the weekend sightseeing, so take some time this morning to do some "flight" seeing aboard a pilot-driven Cessna airplane. **Monterey Bay Aviation** will ferry you on a breathtaking, one-hour scenic flight over the region. Choose a general tour or one that is more specific. For example, if the beauty of Big Sur is your preference, you can soar above Point Lobos, Bixby Bridge, the Point Sur Lighthouse, and the Redwoods. You may see whales and dolphins as they migrate up and down the coast. The Pebble Beach tour is for golf enthusiasts who will marvel at a bird's eye view of one of the world's most famous fairways. No doubt you'll have some stellar photo opportunities while in flight. *Info*: www.montereybayaviation.com. Tel. 831/375-2359. Monterey Airport, 514 Airport Way. $225 for two passengers and $250 for three passengers.

After your flight, find your-self grounded at **Point Lobos State Reserve**. The entrance, located about three miles south of Carmel off Highway 1, is where you'll begin. The park opens daily at 9am and closes a half hour after sunset. Half of the reserve is located on land and this is where you'll find rugged hiking trails and picnic areas. There are sched-uled guided walking tours with times posted at the en-trance, plus two museums: **The Whalers Cabin Museum** and **The Whaling Station Museum**. The former was  built by Chinese fisherman in the 1850s, and the latter is housed in a former garage and offers up displays of harpoons and whaling tools used by the Portuguese seaman who operated The Carmel Bay Whaling Company from 1862-1879.

The rest of the reserve is located beneath the water's surface, but is accessible to scuba divers. Touted as one of the richest marine habitats throughout the state, its menagerie of animals and plants are fully protected by state law from any outside disturbances. Divers are permitted to explore Whalers and Bluefish Coves, but must show proof of certification. If you're thinking of diving, you need to make a reservation in advance as days fill up quickly. *Info*: http://pt-lobos.parks.state.ca.us/Information.htm. Tel. 831/624-8413. Highway 1 three miles south of Carmel. $8 per car entrance fee.

Make your way to downtown Monterey and head to **The Crown & Anchor** (www.crownandanchor.net, Tel. 831/649-6496. 150 West Franklin), a charming pub located below street level. Most of the fare is strictly British, but there are some dishes fit for a Yank as well. It's very casual, but very authentic and kids are welcome, too. The selection of beer is equally impressive. Conclude your weekend by watching the sunset over Monterey Bay from the end of Fisherman's Wharf or, perhaps, perched on a rock near the water's edge reflecting on your fantastic Central Coast weekend.

A WONDERFUL WEEK ALONG THE CENTRAL COAST

The Central Coast is so breathtaking that after a week you'll never want to leave. While you're here you'll have a chance to explore some well known and more obscure spots, **take advantage of the great outdoors**, do some wine tasting if you choose and, whenever possible, be thankful that you've had an opportunity to visit one of the state's most pristine regions.

RECOMMENDED PLAN: With a week to spend along the **Central Coast**, you can easily break up your trip into three mini trips with two nights in **Santa Cruz**, two nights along the **Monterey Peninsula**, a night to relax in **Big Sur**, and a final two nights spent in **Cambria** where you'll visit **Hearst Castle**. You'll want to follow my *One Day* and *Weekend* itineraries that cover Monterey and Carmel with snippets of Big Sur and the surrounding areas. While in **Big Sur**, you'll want to relax, explore the outdoors, and visit the **Henry Miller Memorial Library**. Once in **Cambria**, you'll enjoy the small town ambiance that this village has to offer just miles from what some may consider the behemoth of America – **Hearst Castle**. As you cruise along Highway 1, motoring from destination to destination, you'll pass and perhaps stop at some of the small seaside villages, such as **Moss Landing**, for a rest, bite to eat, or to enjoy the scenery.

Santa Cruz
Situated on the northern part of the Monterey Bay, about 74 miles south of San Francisco and 30 miles from San Jose, **Santa Cruz** is the quintessential beach community. Its main attractions are its

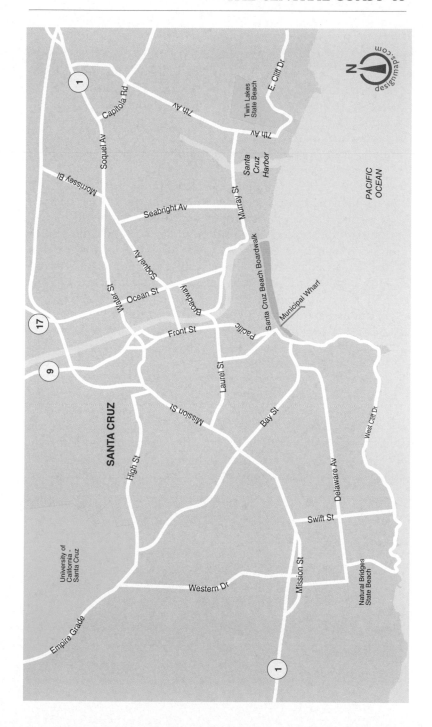

Use San Jose's Airport

If you're flying to the Central Coast, I recommend you land and depart from **San Jose International Airport**. It's about a 45 minute, mostly scenic, drive from the airport to Santa Cruz. From Cambria, your final Central Coast destination, it's about a three hour drive back to the airport. If you have an early flight, skip a night in Big Sur and spend your last night in San Jose. Slumber at **The Fairmont San Jose** (Tel. 408/998-1900) in the center of town, which is within walking distance to many restaurants and venues, and still only a few minutes by car to the airport.

surf, sand and boardwalk, which bodes well for those looking for a lazy and leisurely escape. **Downtown Santa Cruz** offers a bit of charm, and for outdoorsy types there is plenty of hiking, biking, sailing, kayaking and fishing opportunities.

The **Santa Cruz Beach Boardwalk** is one of the few vintage seaside amusement parks still standing in California. It's also home to the **Giant Dipper**, a historic wooden roller coasters that remains as thrilling today as it did when it opened in 1924. The Giant Dipper is one of two such roller coasters left in the state (the other Giant Dipper, also hailing from the 1920s, can be found at Belmont Park in San Diego's Mission Beach neighborhood). The Boardwalk, which played a pivotal role in the 1987 film *Lost Boys*, is also home to a 1911 carousel complete with a menagerie of prancing hand-carved wooden

horses and the long-forgotten brass ring. Other attractions include a log ride, haunted house, arcade games, and much more. Check out **Neptune's Kingdom**, also located here, which features a gigantic indoor family amusement center and a two-story miniature golf course. *Info*: www.beachboardwalk.com. Tel. 831/423-5590. Free admission; rides and games priced independently.

The **Municipal Wharf** (Tel. 831/420-6025), also located just a sandal-toss from the Boardwalk, is lined with mostly touristy shops and restaurants. You can crab and fish from here or, better yet, visit **Stagnaro's** (Tel. 831/427-2334), which operates both fishing and seasonal whale-watching trips.

Santa Cruz, which has declared war on Huntington Beach, California (located several hundred miles south

Surfin' Santa Cruz

Need to get your hands on a surfboard? Try renting one at **Cowell's Beach 'n' Bikini Surf Shop** at 109 Beach Street (Tel. 831/427-2355) or take a lesson from the pros at **Club Ed Surf School** on Cowell Beach (www.club-ed.com. Tel. 831/464-0177). Club Ed offers both private and group lessons.

in Orange County) for the title of Surf City, is known for its laidback attitude and fabulous beaches. Along **West Cliff Drive** is a favorite surfing spot known as **Steamer Lane**. Here pro surfers compete for the best waves. Further down West Cliff Drive is **Natural Bridges State Beach**, with its large sandy swath complete with tide pools, hiking trails and one of the largest colonies of monarch butterflies. These winged beauties cluster together in nearby eucalyptus groves to mate. Another beach worth checking out is **Bonny Doon** (at Bonny Doon Road and Highway 1), a popular and generally less crowded surfing spot located at the end of a steep walkway. If you're not a surfer and don't care to observe others enjoying the sport, then do a little sunning at **Twin Lakes State Beach** where you can also access Schwann Lagoon and avail yourself to its bird-watching opportunities.

Santa Cruz Harbor offers plenty of nautical distractions, including boat rentals, open-boat fishing, and seasonal whale watching excursions. Even if you're a landlubber at heart and have no intention of venturing out onto the high seas, the harbor is worthy of a visit just to do a little window shopping or grab a bit to eat at one of the local grottos. *Info*: www.santacruzharbor.org. Tel. 831/475-6161. 135 Fifth Avenue.

The Drive from Santa Cruz to the Monterey Peninsula
From Santa Cruz, you'll motor down Highway 1, which hugs the ocean. Without stops it will take you about an hour, but why not pull off at one or more of the seaside towns for a look around? **Moss Landing**, which is one of the first communities you'll encounter when you cross over into Monterey County, has 100 residents at the most. This quaint, historic fishing village is known as a place to sleuth for antiques. You'll find everything from dusty, dented heirlooms to more coveted treasures, such as silver serving pieces from the old Del Monte Hotel. On the last Sunday of July, 200 dealers from all over the west converge on the town to take part in the **Moss Landing Antique Fair**. If you're hungry, stop by **Phil's Fish Market** , lauded by the likes of *Sunset* magazine, the *San Francisco Chronicle*, and the *Food Network*. Phil's is open daily from 8:30am to 8pm. *Info*: www.philsfishmarket.com. Tel. 831/ 633-2152. Moss Landing, 7600 Sandholtd Road.

Moss Landing sits at the mouth of the **Elkhorn Slough** (pronounced "slew"), an estuary considered to be one of the nation's rarest ecological systems. At high tide, the Pacific Ocean gushes to the estuary where sea otters, seals, great blue herons and snowy egrets, curlews and sandpipers have made their homes. *Info*: www.elkhornslough.org.

Monterey Peninsula
The one day and weekend itineraries in this chapter truly cover the best the Monterey Peninsula has to offer, so refer to those sections for visits to the **Monterey Bay Aquarium, Fisherman's Wharf, Mission Carmel,** the **National**

Steinbeck Museum, Carmel, Cannery Row, Downtown Monterey, the **Butterfly Sanctuary** and more.

Another stop that should be worked into your itinerary is the storied **Tor House**. Poet Robert Jeffers and his wife Una built their Hobbit-style dwelling on a breathtaking bluff overlooking the Pacific Ocean after moving to Carmel in 1914. Construction on the stone home, which was fashioned after a Tudor barn in England, began in 1918 on the small, low-slung abode. Once complete, the poet-builder began work on **Hawk Tower** in 1920. Utilizing wooden planks and a block and tackle system to transport the stones, Jeffers built the entire tower by himself and used it as a retreat for his wife and a fairy tale annex for his sons. Almost all of his works were done during his time at Tor House, where he was surrounded by granite walls and the beauty of the Carmel coast. He and Una also entertained many luminaries here as well, from photographer Ansel Adams to entertainer extraordinaire Charlie Chaplin to novelist Sinclair Lewis. *Info*: www.torhouse.org. Tel. 831/624-1813. Carmel, 26304 Ocean View Avenue. Adults $7, Students $2 – advanced reservations required. Docent-led tours are available hourly on Fridays and Saturdays only from 10am-3pm, and children under 12 are not permitted.

Big Sur
As you travel south on Highway 1 from Carmel, you'll very quickly happen upon **Big Sur**, the nearly 100-mile stretch of coastline cradled between Carmel and San Simeon near Hearst Castle. The drive can be slow and, at times, treacherous, but never boring. The road toys with travelers with its hairpin turns, stomach-plunging dips, and narrow bridges, all of which seem to teeter along a series of ocean bluffs, cliffs and heady promontories.

The **Bixby Bridge**, one of the area's most famed manmade landmarks, is located about 15 miles from Carmel and is one of the world's highest, single-span concrete bridges.

It rises more than 260 feet above Bixby Creek Canyon and offers panoramic views from various observation areas. The bridge is iconic and seems to convey how truly isolated Big Sur is from the rest of California. Cresting in the distance is **Point Sur Lighthouse**, which sits more than 360 feet above the ocean on a volcanic rock. Built in 1889, four keepers and their families staffed the lighthouse and its fog signal 24 hours a day. The trail to Monterey was long and treacherous making trips few and far between. The U.S. Lighthouse Service provided the keepers with a horse and wagon to retrieve mail and supplies from Pfeiffer's Resort, which is now **Pfeiffer Big Sur State Park**. Each family was given a garden to grow fresh vegetables along with a bulk supply of coal, firewood and other essentials. As the years passed, subsequent lighthouse keepers were privy to better conditions and more modern conveniences. The last keeper vacated the premises in 1974. Listed on the National Register of Historic Places, the unique stone lighthouse continues to guide ships with its now automated light, and restoration has been completed on many of the buildings.

Tours of the lighthouse last three hours and require a steep half-mile climb both ways. Tours are available year-round on weekends with additional days added during the summer. If you're up for it, take a moonlight tour on selected evenings from April to October. *Info*: www.pointsur.com. Tel. 831/625-4419. Point Sur State Historic Park. Adults $8, children $4.

Nepenthe, one of the area's famed restaurants, is a nice place to pull over. Legend has it that the owners' grandparents bought the place from Rita Hayworth and Orson Welles. The two celebrities were traveling from San Francisco back to Los Angeles in 1944  when they found a cabin overlooking the south coast. Entranced, they put a down payment of $167 right there on the spot. That was the first and last time the pair ever laid eyes on their cabin. Instead, they sold it in 1947 and it remains in the same family today. The mini com-

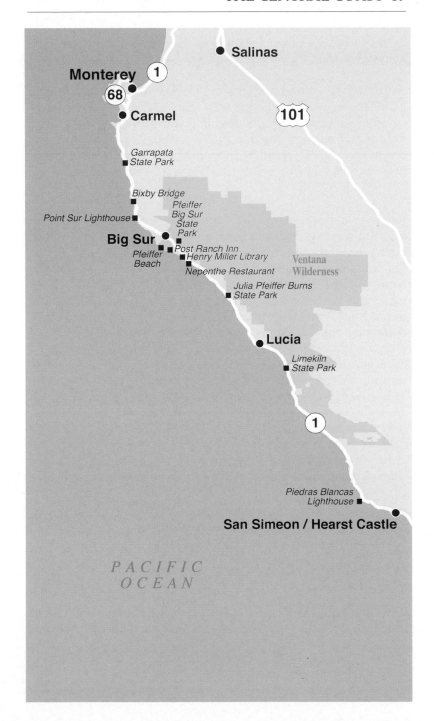

pound includes a pair of restaurants plus a gift shop with unbeliev-able views. *Info*: www.nepenthebigsur.com. Tel. 831/667-2345.

South of Nepenthe on Highway 1 is **Coast Gallery,** designed from large recycled redwood water tanks. The 9,000 square foot complex contains a half-dozen galleries and an espresso bar with indoor and outdoor seating. It also contains original works by renowned artists including paintings by Henry Miller, better known for his controversial prose. *Info*: www.coastgalleries.com. Tel. 831/667-2301.

And speaking of Henry Miller...the writer/artist settled in Big Sur in 1940 after returning from Europe and lived here until 1962 when he moved south to Los Angeles. Miller's ashes were returned to Big Sur upon his death in 1980 and scattered over the region. The **Henry Miller Memorial Library,** less than a half-mile from Nepenthe, is a hybrid gathering spot. Created by longtime Miller friend Emil White (the library is actually White's former home), here you'll find Mr. Miller's books and artwork on display along with a permanent collection of first editions. This is as much a library as it is a salon where artists gather and members of the community congregate to enjoy concerts, readings and exhibitions. You'll want to enjoy some time in the sculpture garden or sit around one of the tables on the lawn to take in the surroundings. *Info*: www.henrymiller.org. Tel. 831/667-2574. Big Sur. Located half-way between Nepenthe and Deetjen's Big Sur Inn in a redwood grove on the mountain side of the road. Open Thursday-Sunday 11am-6pm; everyday during the summer except Tuesday. Free admission.

If you prefer to take advantage of the beauty of Big Sur, head to **Julia Pfeiffer Burns State Park**, named for a well respected, Big Sur pioneering woman. The park stretches from the coastline into the nearby ridges, and features a forest of trees and an 80-foot waterfall that gushes from majestic granite cliffs into the ocean below. This is one of the most pristine stretches of coastline with a 1700-acre underwater reserve that is a paradise for scuba divers. The park is located a few miles south of the Henry Miller Library. *Info*: www.parks.ca.gov.

The Drive from Big Sur to Cambria

This drive is mostly scenic and isolated. It will take you about two hours without stops. About seven miles north of San Simeon is **Piedras Blancas,** named for a trio of rocks located just off shore. In 1990 a small colony of elephant seals set up camp here; now there are thousands of these creatures that can be eagerly viewed from the boardwalk. The 1874 **Piedras Blancas Lighthouse** is also open for monthly tours held on a selected Saturdays. *Info*: Tel. 805/927-6811. As you continue to work your way south to Cambria you will see **Hearst Castle** looming several miles away on your left.

Cambria / Hearst Castle

Located six miles south of Hearst Castle, this quaint hamlet is an ideal base for planning a day trip to the great estate. Cambria is trisected into distinct districts. The East Village, located about two miles from the coast and flanked with gorgeous Victorian homes, forms part of the town center where Main Street crosses Burton Drive (*see photo below*) and Bridge Street. Here you'll find many art galleries, specialty shops, bookstores and restaurants. The town's West Village, situated around Main Street but closer to the ocean, is also lined with similar venues. Completing the trio is **Moonstone Beach**, accessible via Moonstone Drive which follows the coast on a scenic loop that mimics Highway 1. This is where many of the town's waterfront inns and restaurants are located, as well as the pebbled beach and pounding surf.

Cambria is charming, but the main attraction in these parts is **Hearst Castle**. Located halfway between Los Angeles and San Francisco, Hearst Castle is one of the largest historic house museums in the United States. Designed by famed architect Julia Morgan for newspaper mogul William Randolph Hearst, the "little home" that Hearst envisioned ended up being an extravagant 165-room mansion with 127 acres of gardens, terraces, pools and walkways. The collaboration between Morgan and Hearst began in 1919, and "La Cuesta Enchanted" – The Enchanted Hill – was finally completed in 1947. After Hearst's death, the estate was donated to the People of the State of California in 1957. Today the California State Parks Department does an incredible job at keeping the estate looking like a private residence. There are five tours available with each one lasting approximately two hours; a little longer if you include the five-mile bus trip up the hill. You will likely only have time for one tour, maybe two, and advanced reservations are required.

Tour 1 is recommended for first-time visitors and takes you to some of the gardens, through the 18-room guesthouse, the Neptune and Roman pools, and the main house. **Tour 2** will give you a closer look at the main home's upper floors, Hearst's private

suite, the libraries and the kitchen. **Tours 3 & 4** take you to additional gardens, residential quarters, the wine cellar, and terraces. **Tour 5** is a special tour that allows you to see the castle at night. Each tour, which is subject to change due to renovation conditions, reveals architectural gems and numerous works of priceless art. *Info*: www.hearstcastle.com. Reservations required: Tel. 800/444.4445. San Simeon. Tours 1-4 are offered several times daily from 8:40am-4:40pm; Tour 5 is a seasonal tour offered March-May and September-December from 6:30-8:10pm.

If you're spending two days in Cambria, head a bit inland and explore the **Paso Robles wineries**, which are starting to make a name for themselves. Take Highway 1 south a few miles and then head east on Highway 46. Paso Robles is about 30 miles inland. While en route on Highway 46, you'll pass many wineries or see signs directing you to others off the main road. A few stops along the way include **Eberle Winery, EOS Estate Winery at Arciero Vineyards, Firestone** and **Meridian Vineyards**, just to name a few. What I personally like about wine tasting in Paso Robles is that this is one of the few wine growing regions in California that still offers **complimentary tastings** and it remains a best-kept secret despite the fact that the region has been producing wine for

Stay in Paso Robles

If an afternoon in Paso Robles doesn't seem enough, delete one night from my recommended itinerary and add it to your trip here. My hotel recommendations for Paso Robles are **Hotel Cheval** (www.hotelcheval.com, Tel. 805/226-9979, 1021 Pine Street), an incredibly luxe destination near the town square with just 16 rooms that cater to couples; **Villa Toscana** (www.myvillatoscana, Tel. 805/238-5600, 4230 Buena Vista), an intimate inn nestled among the vineyards; and the historic **Paso Robles Inn** (www.pasoroblesinn1.com., Tel. 805/322-7013, 1103 Spring Street), situated in town and well equipped for families.

decades. The small crowds make it easy to avail yourself to the winemaking process and, more than likely, you will have a chance to chat it up with the winemaker, too. *Info*: Contact the Paso Wine Country Alliance. www.pasowine.com. Tel. 800/549-WINE. You can download a winery map from the organization's website.

After visiting a few wineries, make your way to downtown Paso Robles. Seemingly frozen in time, the quaint district is flanked with a charming town square, stately Victorian buildings, and a refreshing collection of local retailers rather than national chains. Adding to the mix are sidewalk cafes and espresso bars.

6. HIGH SIERRA: YOSEMITE & TAHOE

The **High Sierra region** is one of the state's most breathtaking. While Ansel Adams was able to convey Yosemite's beauty in black and white, it was John Muir, the naturalist and perhaps the first true environmentalist, who brought the magnificence of Lake Tahoe to life with these words: "No temple made with hands can compare with Yosemite."

Yosemite and Lake Tahoe, though geological wonders, are vastly different from one another. **Yosemite**, known as the "Crown Jewel" of America's National Parks, is a mass of granite peaks and plunging valleys punctuated with gigantic sequoia trees that climb towards the heavens. **Lake Tahoe**, an azure lake surrounded by snow-sifted mountain peaks, is nevertheless more Manola than granola — or at least Ugg-worthy — with its cache of upscale lodges, selection of finer restaurants, and chatty après-ski destinations.

Ansel Adams did a superb job of capturing the Golden State's High Sierra on film. With each thoughtful angle and calculated click of the camera, Adams revealed the magic that only Mother Nature could conjure up over the course of many hundreds of thousands of years. But let's face it, nothing is quite as arresting as seeing Yosemite's **Half Dome** — or scaling it — out of the frame and in person.

Accommodations in Yosemite are mostly rustic, which is expected in a region sculpted by the Ice Age, but there are a few refined gems for those who have a desire to luxuriate. The gateways leading into the park are surrounded by rural towns that harken back to a gentler era.

Lake Tahoe is equally alluring. But, unlike Yosemite, Tahoe, as it's more commonly referred, has a personality disorder due to its location on the California-Nevada Stateline. On the one side there are some stunning ski resorts coupled with some back-to-basics activities, such as hiking, fishing and boating. Wide open spaces, spectacular state parks and forests, and meandering trails also exist. Cross over the border and you'll encounter glittery casinos, buffet dining, and headlining acts for after-dark entertainment – not that the Nevada side isn't without plenty of outdoor beauty. Many of Tahoe's towns in both states have been subjected to recent developments resulting in luxury condos, plush resorts, and roads that are now more well-traveled.

ONE GREAT DAY IN YOSEMITE

With so much to see, yet so little time, you'll need to pace yourself on this whirlwind trip to what seems like the ends of the earth. Be prepared to walk, hike, explore and reflect on your glorious surroundings.

Before you put the pedal to the metal, be sure to load up on film or delete images from your digital camera – don't forget to carry extra batteries, too. You won't want to miss a single photo opportunity and, believe me, there are plenty of them. Start your journey early. Pack a Thermos of coffee and began your trek along **Highway 41** — ideal if you're staying in Oakhurst — and get ready for your first photo opportunity. Here, just north of Wawona and south of the Valley Floor is **Tunnel View**. The name exists because it is the first real view of the valley motorists witness upon exiting the tunnel. This is an excellent spot to snap a breathtaking shot of the valley in all its panoramic glory. There are two parking areas, so be sure to drive slow as pedestrians are mingling about admiring the beauty.

Continue onward and into the Valley. Your next stop is the misty **Bridalveil Fall**, which offers spectacular views of both the famed **El Capitan** and the falls themselves (*photo at right*). Once you reach the heart of the Valley, you can park at one of the day-use lots and take the **free shuttle** bus to the **Val-ley Visitor Center** in **Yosemite Village**. Mosey next door to the **Ansel Adams Gallery** for some photographic inspiration. Be sure to visit the **Yosemite Museum**, also located near the Visitor Center, which has displays that interpret the history of the native Miwok and Paiute people from 1850 to the present. Check out the ongoing demonstrations, from basket weaving to beadwork, as well as the reconstructed Indian Village of Ahwahnee located behind the museum.

The **Yosemite Cemetery**, a historic place of burial, is located across the street and is the final resting place of many Native Americans, a few park visitors, and those who played an instrumental role in the development of Yosemite. You can borrow or purchase a guide from the Visitor Center.

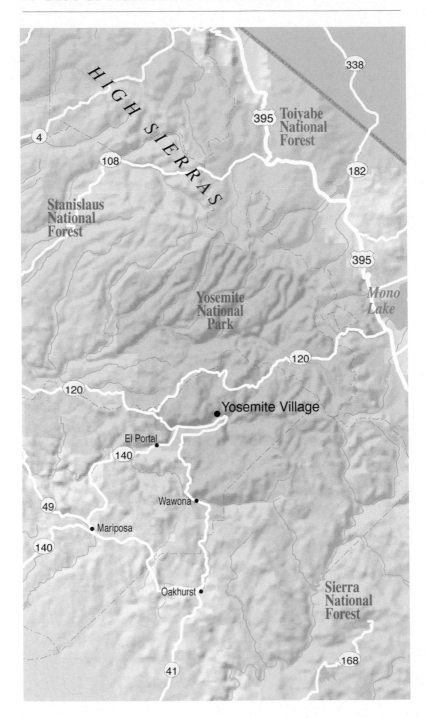

ALTERNATIVE PLAN
Get out there and take a hike to the base of **Bridalveil Fall**. This easy trek is **about a half-mile round-trip** and takes about 20 minutes. Leashed pets are allowed, and children can enjoy the hike as well. Begin at the parking area marked Bridalveil Fall, and follow the paved path that leads from the parking area to the base of the waterfall. The water, regardless of the season, flows year-round. If visiting in the spring or early summer expect some added sprays headed your way. In winter, expect icy conditions that may not be suitable for very young children. After your hike, follow the same trail back to the parking area.

Next, board the free shuttle for a trip around the valley floor, a ride that lasts about an hour if you stay aboard the entire time. While on the valley floor, why not take a one-mile hike to **Lower Yosemite Falls?** Exit the shuttle at stop #6 to begin your adventure at Lower Yosemite Fall Trailhead. This is a short, easy walk with spectacular views of both Upper and Lower Yosemite Falls. Because the falls are mostly snow fed, they tend to gush in spring and early summer before experiencing a dry spell from late July through October. The 30-minute hike is okay for leashed pets and half of loop is also wheelchair accessible.

Other places to exit the shuttle include shuttle stop #16 where the **Nature Center at Happy Isles** is located. This family-oriented venue features exhibits of natural history with an emphasis on wildlife. Nearby are short trails that focus on the area's quartet of environments: forest, river, talus, and fen. Evidence of the 1996 rock fall from the Glacier Point cliff can be viewed from this vantage point as well. The nature center is open May through September.

By now you've probably worked up an appetite. For an unforgettable meal, take the shuttle to stop #3 and make your way to the dining room at the elegant **Ahwahnee Hotel**. Dine beneath a 34-foot-high beamed ceiling while enjoying spectacular views beyond the floor-to-ceiling windows. White linens, fine china and a savory menu complete the experience.

Know Before You Go

• **Highway 41**, also known as Wawona Road, is open year-round but chains may be required during the winter months due to snow conditions.

• The maximum length for single vehicles is 45-feet.

• If you plan on spending the night either at a lodge or campground you will likely need to **make reservations months in advance**.

• There is a seven-day cancellation policy at most hotels and campgrounds. You could snag a coveted room or campsite at the last minute.

• **Fill up before you enter the park** because you won't find a gas station within the confines of Yosemite.

• Vehicles pay an **entrance fee of $20 per car**, which is valid for seven days and includes all vehicle occupants.

• If arriving on foot, horseback, or motorcycle, the cost is $10 per person; free for those 15 years old or younger.

• Tioga Road, Glacier Point Road and Mariposa Grove Road are closed during the winter months.

ALTERNATIVE PLAN
Skip the Ahwahnee Hotel for lunch (maybe consider it for dinner instead – but make a reservation) and take the **El Capitan Shuttle Bus**, which operates mid-June through Labor Day. You can catch it at the Visitor Center (stop #5) on the hour and half hour. Before you catch the shuttle pay a visit to **Degnan's Deli** in Yosemite Village for a made-to-order picnic lunch, which you can enjoy in the shadow of El Capitan at the designated picnic area. Be sure to bring plenty of water regardless of whether you plan to do any climbing or hiking near or around El Capitan.

End your day by watching the sunset on **Half Dome** from **Sentinel Bridge**, shuttle stop #11, and enjoy an early evening ranger-led program. Afterwards, make your way back to your vehicle and depart Yosemite Valley with perhaps one final stop at El Capitan meadow to watch the last rock climbers make their final descent.

A FANTASTIC LAKE TAHOE WEEKEND

A weekend in **Lake Tahoe**, whether you stay on the North Shore or its southern counterpart, can be either romantic if you're a traveling twosome or a fun family escape if you're doing some multi-generational vacationing or just traveling with the kids. Most of your time will be spent **outdoors** enjoying nature with hikes, biking and cruising on the lake. If you're feeling lucky, you can sneak over to the Nevada side and gamble at one of the **casinos**. Either way, you'll emerge a winner having spent a couple of relaxing days in Lake Tahoe.

Friday evening

Arrive a few hours before sunset and check into the **Black Bear Inn**, a romantic luxury lodge with five guestrooms and three free-standing cottages located on a wooded patch in South Lake Tahoe (see details in the *Best Sleeps & Eats* chapter). In the late afternoon, get in the car and motor towards **Heavenly Resort** for a gondola ride. Be sure to arrive before the 4pm closing. Take the eight-passenger, glass enclosed gondola up to the viewing platform or to the top to enjoy a million-dollar sunset. The 2.4 mile trip is $28 adults, $18 for kids ages 5-12 and free for those under 5. *Info*: www.heavenlyresort.com. Tel. 775/586-7000. Heavenly, Nevada, 3860 Saddle Road.

ALTERNATIVE PLAN

The Black Bear Inn isn't suited for children, so if you're traveling with young ones let me recommend **The Village at Squaw Valley USA** (see *Best Sleeps & Eats* chapter), which are self-contained condos ranging in size from studio lofts to three-bedroom hideaways. Even though this is on the North Shore, you can still follow the Friday night itinerary. Instead of the Fremont Bistro & Wine Bar, drive back to the North Shore. Once you arrive back at The Village, head to the **Fireside Pizza Company** (www.firesidepizza.com. Tel. 530/584-6150. Olympic Valley, 1985 Squaw Valley Road) on the premises. Eat at the restaurant or get your pie to go and enjoy a slice within the confines of your cozy abode.

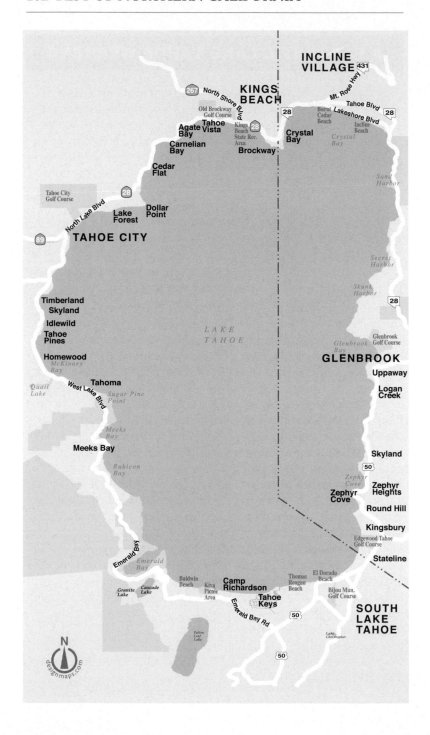

Once the sun goes down and you've descended the mountain, enjoy a cozy dinner at **The Fremont Bistro & Wine Bar.** This stylish dining destination features eclectic tapas, a nice wine selection and a fleet of taps pouring handcrafted beer. *Info*: www.fremontbistro.com. Tel. 530/541-6603. South Lake Tahoe, 1041 Fremont Avenue.

Return to the Black Bear Inn and enjoy a nightcap in front of the lodge's roaring fireplace. Sink into the sofa and plot your next day's adventure before turning in for the night.

Saturday
Start your morning with a full breakfast at the inn or at a nearby café. Visit a nearby deli or grocer and fill a backpack with edibles to enjoy later. Head to **Emerald Bay State Park,** located 22 miles south of Tahoe City.

Designated a National Natural Landmark in 1969, Emerald Bay boasts panoramas of soaring mountains and glacier-carved granite. Besides the obvious natural beauty, the park also features **Vikingsholm**, which is considered one the western hemispheres stellar examples of Scandinavian architecture. This former private estate features a sod roof covering the north and south wings, hand-painted ceilings, a half-dozen fireplaces, and much of the original furnishing intermingled with some undetectable reproductions. Its location on **Fannette Island**, the only island found in all of Lake Tahoe, is also unique. The island is closed from February to mid June due to the nesting of Canadian geese on the land mass. Because there are no predators to speak of, as many as 100 geese can be seen on or near the island by early spring. *Info*: Tel. 530/541-3030. $5 Adults, $3 children. Open daily from 10am to 4pm from Memorial Day to Labor Day.

After your tour of Vikingsholm, enjoy that picnic lunch you've been carrying on a patch of grass overlooking the lake. The stone structure on the top of the island was once a tea house and was built during the late 1920s during the same time that Vikingsholm was constructed. In recent years vandals have left their mark on the rustic tea house and, sadly, only the stone shell has survived.

Designated an underwater state park in 1994, **Emerald Bay** is considered a resting place for countless boats, launches and barges that graced the lake during the 19th century. Most of the craft that sits idle below the water's surface was used during the construction of Vikingsholm. Scuba diving is permitted, and what you'll find several feet below among the abandoned water-craft are trees that are thousands of years old.

Depart Emerald Bay and head towards the North Shore to **Cal-Neva Resort** in Crystal Bay on the Nevada side. The resort actually straddles the state line making it possible to do the backstroke from Nevada to California in the resort's swimming pool. The resort was originally built in 1926 and rebuilt a decade later in just one month after it was destroyed by fire.

A trip to Cal-Neva is like visiting vintage Tahoe, but not for long. Rumor has it that a major renovation will result in a very different Cal-Neva than the one **Frank Sinatra** and his Rat Pack fre-quented. In fact, Sinatra briefly owned the resort from 1960 to 1963. While on property, take a peek in the Frank Sinatra Celeb-rity Showroom which houses the Mural Story of entertainment. Cal-Neva is also the site of the state's largest bronze sculpture, Chief Joseph. After you've conducted your own self-guided tour, retreat to the resort's famed Circle Bar to enjoy the spectacular views from beneath the **Crystal Dome**, which boasts some 7,000 pieces of hand-cut German crystal. Grab a chair at the command-ing circular bar, and enjoy a full menu and every libation imag-inable. Afterwards, try your luck in the casino or head back to your inn for a relaxing evening.

If you happen to be at the resort on a Friday or Saturday evening at 7pm, take a **scheduled walking tour** of Cal-Neva. Highlights include visits to **Marilyn Monroe's cabin**, underground tunnels and tales off famous and restless apparitions. *Info*: www.calnevaresort.com. Tel. 800/233-5551. Crystal Bay, Nevada, 2 Stateline Road. Tours are $8 and last about 40 minutes.

Sunday

Plan to rise early for a trip aboard a **hot-air balloon**. You'll launch from the Tahoe Flyer, a 21 ton, two-deck, catamaran-style aircraft carrier vessel designed and built to inflate and launch hot-air balloons. The adventure begins shortly after sunrise, where a continental breakfast is served on board the **Tahoe Flyer**. You'll witness the inflation process from the

ALTERNATIVE PLAN
If you arrive in Lake Tahoe during the winter, pass on Emerald Bay and instead try something other than skiing: **dogsledding**. These Husky-driven dogsled sojourns originate from Sugar Bowl and the Resort at Squaw Creek. *Info*: Wilderness Adventures, Tel. 530/550-8133. Tours last approximately one hour.

upper deck, board the inflated carrier, and enjoy a one-hour flight above Lake Tahoe. On some days visibility is so clear that it's possible to view the peaks of Yosemite some 150 miles away. At the end of the flight, participants join the crew in a Champagne toast and round of mimosas. *Info*: www.laketahoeballoons.com. Tel. 800/872-9294. $250 per person. Flights are May through October. The entire experience takes about four hours from start to finish.

Use T.A.R.T.

Tahoe has a rather extensive transportation system known as **T.A.R.T.**, short for the Tahoe Area Regional Transportation. Free shuttles are available at night so you don't have to worry about drinking and driving. *Info*: www.laketahoetransit.com. Tel. 530/550-1212.

Drive towards Truckee to visit **Donner Memorial State Park** and its **Emigrant Trail Museum**. Within the walls is a depiction of the area's history and the people. Beside the Native Americans, you'll also learn of the Donner Party, the infamous group of California-bound American settlers stranded for six winter months, from late 1846 to early 1847, at what is now known as Donner

Lake during their futile attempt to reach the Pacific Ocean. Take a self-guided tour, and be sure to watch the 30 minute movie on the Donner Party playing hourly. *Info*: www.parks.ca.gov. Tel. 530/582-7892. Truckee. Donner Pass Road. Open daily 9am-4pm.

Afterward, prowl around historic **Downtown Truckee**. The town retains an Old West flair and is filled with shops, restaurants and a few galleries. While here, have dinner at **Dragonfly Restaurant & Sushi Bar**, which is wildly popular with locals. The restaurant offers a Pan-Asian menu, selection of sushi and full bar. Open for dinner Wednesday-Monday from 5:30-9:30pm. Such a great way to end a fantastic weekend in Lake Tahoe! *Info*: Tel. 530/587-0557. Truckee, 10118 Donner Pass Road.

Winter Fun in Tahoe

• Get a real workout while strapped to a pair of **snowshoes**.
• Enjoy an après-ski with a bubbly soak — and a glass of bubbly — in an **outdoor hot tub**.
• Strap on a pair of skates and take to the **outdoor ice rink** at the Resort at Squaw Creek.
• Grab a no-nonsense **saucer or sled** and enjoy an old-fashioned romp in the snow.
• Stay toasty beside Lady Luck and take your chances at the blackjack table inside one of the **Nevada casinos**.

A WONDERFUL WEEK IN THE HIGH SIERRA

Seven days in the High Sierra, if nothing else, will result in an appreciation for nature. It's likely you'll have done some type of outdoor activity, whether it's **hiking, skiing, snowshoeing** or **rock climbing**. The drive from Yosemite to Lake Tahoe will also reveal some of California's lesser known towns that are rich in historiy and offer a few interesting venues. Though the High Sierra region conjures up images of rugged terrain, and rightly so, there are some luxurious finds as well. Whether you're hiking to the top of Yosemite's **Half Dome** or jumping moguls on your way downhill from one of Tahoe's pristine ski resorts, a trip to the High Sierra is an exhilarating and memorable experience.

RECOMMENDED PLAN: With a week to enjoy, I suggest you spend 2-3 nights in **Yosemite** and 4-5 nights in **Lake Tahoe**. You may also want to carve out a night—or two—to spend along the way in one of the region's historic towns. I've included **Sutter Creek**, which is about half-way between Yosemite and Lake Tahoe. You'll want to follow the *One Great Day* itinerary outlined for Yosemite and the *Fantastic Weekend* plan I put together for Lake Tahoe. Both cover a lot of ground for each region. In addition, take a day trip to **Virginia City, Nevada,** while staying in Lake Tahoe. This former mining town, located about 40 miles from Tahoe, is a bit kitschy but interesting nonetheless.

Yosemite
If you have designs at staying at **The Ahwahnee** inside the park (see the *Best Sleeps & Eats* chapter), you'll need to plan well in advance as the hotel is typically booked up to a year in advance. The **Chateau du Serra** in Oakhurst is another great choice—and an opulent one at that—if you're traveling without children. With or without kids, make time for a picnic lunch in the shadow of one of Yosemite's iconic granite cliffs or waterfalls.

Yosemite is open all year. Keep in mind that the park receives most of its precipitation in January, February and March. Summers tend to be hot and dry, while spring and fall are probably the most beautiful seasons — not too mentioned least crowded — for a visit. Don't be surprised if you're enjoying a spectacular sunny day that suddenly turns sullen due to an unexpected and unforeseen thunderstorm. It happens more than you might think.

Incorporating much of the itinerary from One Great Day in Yosemite from this chapter, you'll be able to see many of the park's highlights. Other experiences within Yosemite that shouldn't be missed include the **Mariposa Grove of Big Trees**. Located at the southern end of the park along Highway 41 is one of the park's giant sequoia groves. From here you can hike to the top of the Grizzly Giant or, if you don't feel you're in tip-top shape, take a tram tour instead.

The **Hetch Hetchy Valley and Reservoir** (trying saying that 10 times fast), located on the east side of the park, where naturalist John Muir lost his quarter of a century battle against the government that allowed the creation of a dam to be built that would supply drinking water to the San Francisco Bay area, is a nice stop. You can walk across the dam, hike, and admire the spring wildflowers. **Wapama Falls** and **Tueulala Falls**, two of North America's tallest waterfalls, are located here as well.

Got what it takes to climb **Half Dome**? This is the country's

sheerest cliff and a beacon of beauty for park visitors. Block out an entire day for this 17-mile, round-trip trek and make sure you are in fit condition. Often people misjudge their endurance level, so be careful. The final 400 feet to Half Dome's summit takes place on a staircase secured with cable supports, in place from May to October, that double as handrails. To avoid the crowds and hot weather, plan your hike shortly after the cables are installed, and follow these rules:

- Do your hiking mid-week during late spring or early fall avoiding weekends and summer months if at all possible.
- Bring a pair of leather gloves.
- Don't take a chance with a pair of new shoes; make sure your hiking boots are already broken in for optimum comfort.
- Be sure to bring plenty of water and some easy to carry snacks, such as energy bars and nuts.

If the thought of such a climb leaves you dizzy, you're better off just viewing Half Dome from afar. Glacier Point, Tunnel View, Sentinel Bridge and Mirror Lake all offer spectacular views of Half Dome. If you are a beginning hiker, here are some of Yosemite's easier trails:

- **Bridalveil Fall**, half-mile roundtrip, has a paved

Yosemite Fun Facts

- **Bridalveil Fall** is the equivalent of a 62-story building.
- **Yosemite Falls**, at 2,425 feet, is the tallest waterfall in North America.
- The largest granite monolith on Planet Earth is **El Capitan** (*photo below*).
- Yosemite was **one of the first wilderness parks** in the United States.
- The park covers nearly **1,200 square miles**.
- The park has been designated a **World Heritage Site**.
- More than **3.5 million people** visit Yosemite each year, yet the average visitor experiences only seven square miles.

trail that leads from parking area to the base of the year-round flowing waterfall.

- **Lower Yosemite Falls**, one-mile roundtrip, offers spectacular views of both Upper and Lower Yosemite Falls. The waterfall is typically dry from late July to August.
- **Cook's Meadow Loop**, one-mile roundtrip, offers stunning views of Half Dome, Glacier Point, and Royal Arches.
- **Mirror Lake/Meadow**, two miles roundtrip or a five-mile loop around the lake, where exhibits detail the story of the area's lake-to-meadow transformation. Nice area for spotting wildlife.

Yosemite seems to be a place that is best experienced during daylight. Or is it? Because of its isolated location—virtually miles from any city lights—the ebony night sky is a great place for **stargazing**. If you're like me, you'll try to guess what constellations are what and hope for a falling star or two. But park experts suggest you come prepared with a star chart, flashlight, and binoculars to make the most of your time. During the summer months, would-be astronomers arrive in droves, telescopes in hand, to set up camp at Glacier Point. There are also astronomy walks and talks offered at various locations throughout the park, including **Yosemite Valley, Tuolumne Meadows** and **Wawona**. Inquire at the Visitors Center.

Winter Fun in Yosemite
Yosemite is also a fun place to find yourself in the winter as long as you know activities are limited due weather conditions. You can downhill ski and snowboard at **Badger Pass**, the oldest skiing area in California. Skiing and snowboarding take place daily from 9am-4pm from mid-December through March. There are 10 runs with 85% of the slopes dedicated to beginners and intermediate skiers. *Info*: Tel. 209/362-8430.

It may not be Rockefeller Center, but the **Curry Village Ice Rink**, an outdoor skating rink at Yosemite Valley, is a fun and festive way to spend a cold, sunny afternoon. At the rink is a warming hut, fire pit, vending machines and a rental/retail shop. It's open both days and evenings from mid-November through mid-March. *Info*: Tel. 209/372-8319.

For the most up-to-date information on Yosemite National Park, be it weather or road conditions, directions to one of the landmarks, hotel and campground information or directions to one of the destinations in this chapter, visit www.yosemitepark.com or www.nps.gov/yose. Everything you need to know is available with the click of a mouse.

Sutter Creek
Half way between Yosemite and Lake Tahoe is the Mother Lode town of California's Gold Country: **Sutter Creek**. With a nod to its storied past, the **Gold Rush**, and a toast to its fledgling future, winemaking, Sutter Creek is an ideal place to stop for the night. Just 2 1/2 hours from Yosemite and 2 hours from Lake Tahoe, Sutter Creek is a town that looks as if it is stuck in a Wild West time warp. *Info*: www.suttercreek.org. Tel. 209/267-1344.

To reach Sutter Creek from Yosemite, take Highway 140 to Highway 120 to Old Highway 49. The drive is approximately 125 miles. From Sutter Creek to Lake Tahoe, take Highway 49 to Highway 50 east. You'll travel about 100 miles.

The best way to get acquainted with Sutter Creek is by embarking on a **self-guided walking tour**. You'll stroll past historic homes and buildings hailing from the mid-1800s. Many are still private residences, and others house businesses. At **51 Main Street** is a former drug store whose walls date back to 1850 – the building is now home to an ice cream parlor. The former butcher shop at **59 Main Street** was built around 1888 and is now a bookstore. *Info*: Maps can be downloaded at www.suttercreek.org.

If you're exploring Gold Country, shouldn't you at least take a peek inside a mine? **Sutter Gold Mine**, located north about 15

minutes away on Highway 49, offers hard hat tours, rides aboard the Boss Buggy Shuttle, and the chance to delve deep underground for a tutorial in gold mining. The Gold Theatre next to the mine shows a film on the frenzy of the California Gold Rush. *Info*: Tel. 209/736-2708.

In recent years gold had given way to grappa with more and more wineries sprouting up in Amador County. Do a little tasting while in town at **Avio Vineyards & Winery**. *Info*: www.aviowine.com. Tel. 209/267-1515. 14520 Ridge Road. Open Friday-Sunday 11am-5pm. Or try **Sutter Ridge Vineyards**, owned by a fourth-generation winemaking family. They offer picnic areas and a vineyard tour. *Info*: www.sutterridgewine.com. Tel. 209/267-1316. 14110 Ridge Road. Open Friday-Sunday 11am-4pm.

Main Street and its neighboring avenues are lined with mom and pop gift shops, clothing stores, antique emporiums and eateries. For a fine meal and local flair, check out **Caffe Via d'Oro** at 36 Main Street. Here you'll enjoy a nice meal and a chilled glass of local wine served from behind the copper-cloaked bar. Cross the threshold of the **Sutter Creek Ice Cream Emporium** at 51 Main Street and you've done a little time-travel. Belly up to the soda fountain (it's original) and enjoy a scoop or two with all your favorite toppings.

On nearby **Eureka Street** are a few places worth popping in to, such as **Susan's Place** at 15 Eureka Street which serves food, hosts oenophiles for wine tasting, and sells Sierra Foothill wines as keepsakes. Follow the scent of roasting coffee beans to **Sutter Creek Roasting Company** at 20 Eureka Street for either a caffeinated concoction, fresh-baked scone or both.

You may want to plan you visit around some of Sutter Creek's festive annual events, including **Behind the Cellar Door** held in **February** when the Amador County wineries come together to host two-days of barrel-tasting, food, live music and demonstrations. This wine growing region is still undiscovered by the masses, so check it out before the secret is out. *Info*: www.amadorwine.com. Tel. 209/245-6992.

Relive the Wild West at **Black Bart Hold Up Days** in June. The two-day historic happening takes you back to June of 1883 when Black Bart had his last successful stage coach robbery. Events include historic reenactments, a barbecue and hoedown, and live entertainment.

The **Blues & Brews Garden** gets underway in early **September** and features a pair of beer gardens and live blues. Tickets, just $25 per person, include a commemorative mug, brews and non-alcoholic beverages. *Info:* Tel. 209/267-5317.

Lake Tahoe

If you follow the weekend itinerary that I created for Lake Tahoe, you'll experience an exhilarating gondola ride at sunset from **Heavenly Resort**, admire the wonders of **Emerald Bay State Park** including **Vikingsholm** on Fannette Island, take a self-guided or guided tour of **Cal-Neva Resort** once owned by Frank Sinatra, discover the thrill — or disappointment, depending on how you do! — of Tahoe's **casinos,** enjoy a ride in a hot-air balloon at sunrise, visit **Donner Memorial State Park**, and take a stroll around **Downtown Truckee.** So what's left? Plenty!

Winter Fun in Tahoe

There's no shortage of slopes to conquer in Lake Tahoe. The better resorts and ski conditions are found on the California side. At press time lift tickets averaged $60 adults, $50 for teens, and $10 for children. Rates for seniors are in the neighborhood of $40. On holidays the rates increase by a few dollars. If you're visiting in the winter I suggest you avoid skiing on the weekend and on or near holidays. Try to hit the slopes midweek when others are at work and school.

Considered one of the country's top resorts, **Alpine Meadows** (one of my favorite ski destinations as a college student) is located in Tahoe National Forest and features 2,400 acres, groomed runs, and more than a half-dozen powder bowls. There are 13 lifts for skiers and snowboarders with a base elevation of nearly 7,000 feet. *Info:* www.skialpine.com. Tel. 530/583-4232. Open daily from 9am-4pm November-May. From South Lake Tahoe take Highway 89 north to Alpine Meadows Ski Area near Tahoe City.

Overlooking Tahoe's South Shore is **Heavenly Ski Resort** tucked amid the Sierra Nevada Mountain Range. The mountain is so enormous that it actually spills into Nevada. There are 17 lifts on the California side and 12 lifts in Nevada. Boasting the longest vertical drop in the Tahoe Basin, some five miles long, Heavenly caters to both the novice and the pro skier and snowboarder. *Info:* www.skiheavenly.com. Tel. 775/586-7000. South Lake Tahoe, Corner of Wildwood and Saddle.

The 1960 Olympic Winter Games were held at **Squaw Valley USA**. Not only has it withstood the test of time, it's gotten better with age. Nestled among a half-dozen peaks are 4,000 acres of terrain, and an annual average snow pack of more than 450 inches. Its intricate network of ski lifts, 31 in all, almost guarantees a minimal wait time to ascend to the top. Nearly two-thirds of the runs cater to beginning and intermediate skiers with wide,

open bowls and nicely groomed runs. Advanced and expert runs are some of the best around. Squaw Valley also offers night skiing from 4-9pm, and employs a professional staff of instructors at its ski school. Not in the mood to ski? Try snow tubing instead. *Info:* www.squaw.com. Tel. 530/583-6985. Take Highway 89 north to Squaw Valley.

Sure, everyone wants bragging rights to having skied Heavenly or Squaw Valley, but a one-day ski pass doesn't come cheap. If you're just learning to ski or don't care to spend a lot of money, consider **Granlibakken Ski Resort**. Lift tickets are just $21 for a full day, $12 for a child. It's perfect for beginners and intermediate skiers and snowboarders. Rarely crowded, the intimate recreational area offers cross-country skiing and snowshoeing plus a snow play area with saucer rentals. *Info:* www.granlibakken.com. Tel. 800/543-3221. Tahoe City, 725 Granlibakken Road.

Tahoe's Top Ski Resorts

- Heavenly Ski Resort
- Alpine Meadows
- Squaw Valley
- Kirkwood
- Northstar at Tahoe

Sleigh rides do more than just grace Christmas cards, they actually exist in Lake Tahoe. Take an old-fashioned glide in an antique European sleigh through the woods to view one of Lake Tahoe's spectacular vistas. The cozy two-seater is perfect for couples, but there is also a "party" sleigh that can accommodate up to 20 people. Sleighs are equipped with warm blankets and jingle bells. Dinner sleigh rides also available. *Info:* www.sleighride.com. Tel. 775/588-2953. Stateline, Nevada, 50 Highway 50. $20 adults, $10 children.

Did You Know? ...

- Lake Tahoe is the **second deepest lake** in the U.S. with a depth of 1,645 feet.
- At its longest and widest the lake measures 22 miles by 12 miles
- Its circumference is 72 miles.
- The lake straddles the California-Nevada Stateline with **2/3 in the Golden State** and just 1/3 in Nevada.
- At lake level the annual snowfall averages just 125 inches, but **at alpine elevations the annual snowfall hovers around 600 inches**.

Historic Sites of South Lake Tahoe

Lake Tahoe has some historic and interesting sites, such as Vikingsholm mentioned earlier in this chapter. Among those worthy of a visit is the

Thunderbird Lodge, a once great residential estate built in 1939. Today tours are available by reservation, and visitors must be shuttled to the lodge from the Incline Village/Crystal Bay Visitors Center. *Info:* Tel. 775/832-8750 for reservations.

The **Ehrman Mansion at Sugar Pine Point State Park** was built in 1903 and is a rustically grand three-story house harkening back to Tahoe's era of summer homes. The house is now a museum complete with period-style furnishings. *Info:* (Tel. 530/525-7982. Tahoma. 7595 W. Lake Boulevard.

The **Olympic Museum at High Camp** at Squaw Valley includes both a scenic cable car ride up the mountain and a history lesson once you arrive at the top. Inside is a collection of memorabilia, photos, articles and video presentations detailing the events of the VIII Olympic Winter Games of 1960. It marks the first games held in the Western United States and the first that were televised. *Info:* www.squaw.com. Tel. 530/583-6985. Olympic Valley, 1960 Squaw Valley Road. Open mid-June through September.

Finally, you'll find plenty of biking and walking trails in and around Lake Tahoe, as well as oppotunities to go river rafting, boating, hiking, horseback riding, and shopping. See Chapter 10, *Best Activities*, for details.

Virginia City
Just 40 miles away from Tahoe in Nevada is **Virginia City**, founded in 1859 when two Irishmen discovered gold in Six-Mile Canyon, land also claimed by H.T.P. Comstock. Once word got out that gold was struck, hundreds of prospectors made their way to what they dubbed "Comstock Lode" to mine their own fortunes. Swarthy prospectors emerged millionaires and erected mansions as a tribute to their newfound wealth. **Mark Twain** passed through Virginia City working briefly as a reporter for the local newspaper, a job that launched his writing career.

The mining boom transformed the town into an important settlement between Denver and San Francisco. At its peak, Virginia City was a boisterous and bawdy town fueled by the blessings and curses of the Gold Rush.

These days Virginia City (*see photo below*), America's largest **National Historic Landmark**, is a little kitschy, some might even say tacky, but it makes for an interesting day trip. The entire town is one never-ending attraction with its flair for the Wild West. An enjoyable way to spend time here is to board the **Silver Line Express** locomotive and venture back to 19th-century Nevada. You'll witness 100-mile views across the mountains and high desert, go behind the doors of historic mansions, peak inside abandoned mines, and travel on the V & T railroad following the same route travelers took more than 100 years ago. You'll have a chance to visit shops, enjoy a bite to eat in a tavern or saloon, and take in some live entertainment.

If you're visiting in the fall, see the world-famous **Camel Races** (September) where jockeys straddle the backs of trotting camels, ostriches and emus. In October, the **World Championship Outhouse Races** get underway as three-person teams compete for the title as they race down the main street with wildly decorated outhouses. During the same month there are also tours of the old cemeteries and haunted buildings. Come December its **Christmas on the Comstock**, a month-long celebration featuring a parade of lights, an arts and crafts fair, a gingerbread social, and more.

Info: From Lake Tahoe, take Highway 28 and follow the signs leading to Virginia City. The trip is about 90 minutes from Tahoe City. www.visitvirginiacitynv.com. Tel. 800/719-7587.

7. THE NORTH COAST

One of California's greatest and little known assets is the rugged and rich **North Coast**. The craggy seaboard, heavy fog, desolate highways, and glimpses of grazing elk, coupled with jagged rocks that rise from the ocean floor, are more consistent with the Irish coast than the Golden State. Only the 2,000-year-old giant redwood trees, a familiar and famous site in these parts, offer confirmation.

Ferndale, located in Humboldt County just south of Eureka, is a quaint and nearly unchanged Victorian Village established in 1852. Some 50 miles down the coast is the equally enchanting town of **Mendocino** and neighboring villages and regions, such as Elk, Albion, and the wine-growing region of **Andersen Valley**.

The region starts north of Sonoma and trails upward to the California-Oregon state line. During the 1920s, when road crews were constructing Highway 1, the steep mountains proved to be too much for the men and instead they lopped the road over more manageable hills and merged it with Highway 101 – leaving in their wake a pristine and unspoiled stretch of coast. For that, we and future generations owe them a debt of gratitude.

Ferndale's storefronts and collection of inns has generated state historic landmark status for the entire town (*see photo below*). Because of its authentic appeal, Ferndale is popular with location scouts having appeared in such films as *The Majestic* starring Jim Carrey and *Outbreak* with Dustin Hoffman.

The town of **Mendocino** is a charming Victorian hamlet known for its intimate shops, cozy restaurants and art galleries. While its cluster of Cape Cod-style homes seem to speak to the seafaring days of long ago, its isolated location is what attracted throngs of artists here during the 1950s. Mendocino also was cast as Cabot Cove in the Angela Lansbury television series *Murder She Wrote* with the Blair House bed and breakfast serving as the fictional home of Lansbury's character Jessica Fletcher. The nearby Heritage House was used in the Alan Alda film *Same Time Next Year*.

Although the North Coast is a favorite setting for Hollywood filmmakers, there isn't a trace of tinsel to be found. The serrated coast, deserted headlands, random wildlife, and giant redwood trees, which writer John Steinbeck dubbed the "ambassadors from another time," are such that they simply can't be recreated on some sterile Hollywood soundstage.

ONE GREAT DAY IN FERNDALE

Ferndale, population 1,382, moves at about the same pace it did at the turn-of-the-century – slow and steady. You'll want to stroll about ducking into shops, grabbing a leisurely meal or, perhaps, afternoon tea. The well-preserved buildings, also known as **Butterfat Palaces**, a term coined during the epoch when an abundance of prosperity was fueled by the dairy industry, often look like tiered wedding cakes frosted with ornate turrets, gables and thick posts.

Start your day with breakfast at **Cream City Café**, where you can grab a bagel or pastry and a cup of coffee before getting on with your day. *Info*: Tel. 707/786-4442. 543 Main St. Next, head to the **Ferndale Museum** where you can explore an abundance of artifacts including furniture and items that have survived since the town was founded. Among the relics is an operating seismograph, a telephone switchboard, working crank phones, logging and farming equipment, a barber shop and a complete blacksmith shop. The museum also provides walking tours of Ferndale, which need to be booked in advance. *Info*: Tel. 707/786-4486. 515 Shaw Avenue.

You could also go it on your own with a **self-guided tour**. A free souvenir map, distributed by *The Ferndale Enterprise*, is available at many establishments around town. The map features a slew of historic homes, churches, and Main Street shops, whose edifices date back to the late 19th and early 20th centuries. Many of the false front stores tightly abut one another, fueling rumors of buildings being linked together via secret passages. Main Street eventually becomes Francis Street, home to the 1891 Masonic Temple at 212 whose Eastlake-Stick architecture truly speaks to the era. Adjoining the temple is the 1899 Thomas H. Faulkner House at 230 Francis. Other historic and striking designs are found at 207 and 219 Francis Street.

Combine your historic expedition with a little shopping as you stroll Main Street and its neighboring avenues. Pop into the old-

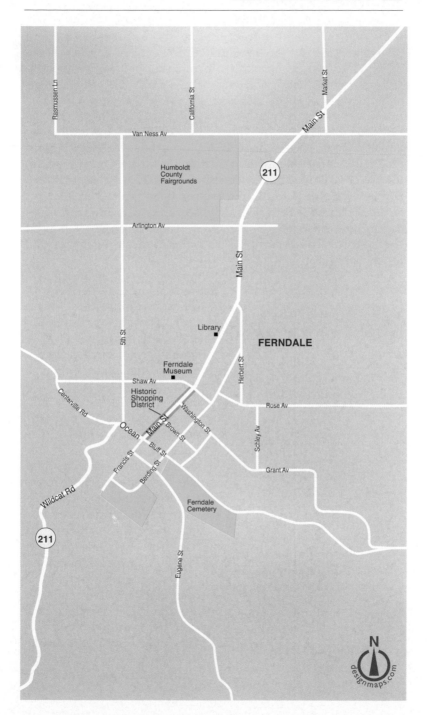

fashioned mercantile stores, antique shops, art galleries, and boutiques. Salivate at the sight of homemade candies being dipped into vats of chocolate, slip into a shop where saddles are still crafted by hand, and enjoy the sound of trotting horses ferrying passengers about town.

Ferndale has some other interesting buildings, including **The Palace Saloon**, housed in a 1902 Victorian false front at 353 Main Street. It holds the distinction of being the farthest tavern west in the lower 48 United States. The **Shaw House**, at 703 Main Street, is the town's oldest building having been erected in 1884 for Ferndale founder Seth Shaw. Subsequent additions, including one in 1866, have been documented. The building once housed the post office and is currently one of the town's premier bed and breakfast inns.

Next, grab a picnic lunch at **La Petite Maison**, and then embark on a nature hike through **Russ Park**. The park features 110 acres, including a closed-canopy forest bird sanctuary complete with three miles of hiking trails. Its location, in the heart of Redwood Country, makes it unique since the park is actually a Sitka Spruce forest – a rarer type of tree than the redwoods that populate the region. The climate within the park is moist, which accounts for the moss-covered logs and curtains of moss that hang from the trees. Have your picnic on the bench overlooking the pond and, should you dare, grab on to the rope swing and dangle above the skunk cabbage scattered across the water. Since this is a bird sanctuary, you'll encounter many feathered friends but other

X-mas in Ferndale

If you can plan your trip to coincide with the winter holidays you'll be in for a real treat. Christmas in Ferndale is likened to a Norman Rockwell painting has come to life. Children decorate **Christmas trees along Main Street**, and the entire town turns out for the merchants-hosted **Hospitality Night**. The fire department, an assembly of volunteers, hang nearly 1000 lights on an enormous Sitka spruce at the end of Main Street as the town gathers for the annual lighting of **America's tallest living Christmas tree**.

wildlife is present, too. Salamanders and frogs are common, as are banana slugs which are found mostly along the trail.

End your day in Ferndale with a romantic carriage ride through town and beyond. Coachwoman Rhonda Hickey, owner of the **Ferndale Horse & Carriage Company**, will ferry you around in style for up to two hours. Reservations are required 48 hours in advance or, you can make arrangements with your innkeeper. *Info:* www.victoriancarriage.com. Tel. 530/635-1628.

A FANTASTIC MENDOCINO WEEKEND

A weekend in **Mendocino** will leave you feeling recharged at the end of your stay. You can explore the charming village and spend some time browsing through shops, or enjoy the great outdoors as you maneuver a kayak through a deserted estuary. **Anderson Valley**, which neighbors Mendocino, allows for a few stolen hours of **wine tasting**. Then there are those moments spent devouring the pages of a good book you've been longing to finish or taking a leisurely hike atop the jagged bluffs. You know that massage you've been promising yourself? Now you finally have some guilt-free time to enjoy it.

Friday evening
It's likely you'll have had a long trek having just flown into San Francisco or Oakland, then making the three hour drive north. So, first things first: check into **Stanford Inn by the Sea** then unwind with a Raindrop Therapy massage at the inn's spa. Order room service, soak in the inn's hot tub, and relax with a bottle of wine under the stars.

Saturday
Wake up and wander down to **Raven's Restaurant** located at the inn, where breakfast is complimentary for overnight guests. Afterwards, hop in the car and head up to **Fort Bragg** where you'll board the **Skunk Train**, touted as one of the 10 most scenic rail trips in North America. The train, which got its nickname

back in 1925 due to the pungent odor the engine's mixture of gasoline and smoke caused, pulls out from the station at 10am and the round-trip excursion lasts about four hours. The Skunk line was built as a logging railroad to haul massive redwood logs to the Mendocino Coast sawmills. The train, which features restored railcars, travels at a leisurely pace averaging 29 miles per hour. The views from the covered cars and observation cars haven't changed in decades. You'll pass towering trees, witness deer drinking from the Noyo River, see an occasional lone cabin tucked in the forest, while chugging through tunnels, across bridges and past open meadows. The train follows the same 1855 redwood coastal route once used to move the massive logs to the sawmills. Food and drink are available on board.

During the summer months the Skunk Train hosts a moveable feast featuring a delicious barbecue picnic among the redwoods. The train also hosts special events throughout the year, including an **Easter Egg Hunt** in spring, the **Wine & Redwoods** excursion in May, and **Oktoberfest** in fall. *Info*: www.skunktrain.com. Tel. 800/866-1690. Fort Bragg Depot (foot of Laurel Street). Adults $47, children $22.

While Fort Bragg isn't quite as picturesque as some of the other coastal towns, it is home to the only public garden in the continental United States directly fronting the ocean. The **Mendocino Coast Botanical Gardens** is truly breathtaking and just a short distance from the train depot. Thunderous waves mist the collection of manicured gardens, while the moist climate keeps the canyons cloaked in ferns. You'll find a dense coastal pine forest, more than 100 species of birds, and the Cliff House where you can take shelter to watch the winter and spring migrations of the

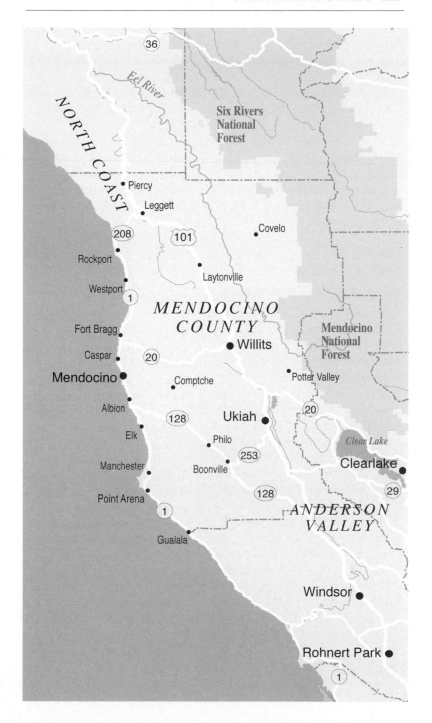

majestic gray whales. In addition to the abundance of flowers that bloom here, there are also 80 varieties of mushrooms that thrive in the moist climate. *Info:* www.gardenbythesea.org. Tel. 707/964-4352. Fort Bragg. 18220 North Highway 1. Adults $10, Children $4. Open daily 9am-4pm; until 5pm March-October.

Afterwards, head to **The Rendezvous** for dinner. Located on Main Street in Fort Bragg, this is one of Mendocino County's highly-acclaimed restaurants. If you want to start making your way back towards Mendocino, skip The Rendezvous and instead dine at **Café Beaujolais** in Mendocino. See Chapter 9, *Best Sleeps & Eats*, for more details.

Afterwards, enjoy a nightcap at the historic Mendocino Hotel and Garden Suites before heading back to your hotel.

ALTERNATIVE PLAN

Not everyone is big on paddling a canoe or kayak. If this sounds like you, bypass this morning adventure and instead start with a visit to the village of Mendocino. Once you've wandered around, hop in the car and follow Highway 128 through the **Anderson Valley** where you'll spend the afternoon **wine tasting**. Grab a picnic lunch in the town of Boonville and enjoy it at the winery of your choice (*see sidebar on page 135*) or along the Navarro River among the redwoods. As you mosey down Highway 128, you'll be heading towards the 101 Freeway which will take you south towards San Francisco or Oakland Airports.

Sunday

After a leisurely breakfast at the hotel, take a canoe or kayak ride down the **Big River**, which is one of the only major undeveloped estuaries in Northern California. The river is punctuated with forested canyons, swimming holes (though it's usually too cold to take a dip) and wildlife. Be sure to check with the hotel first for weather and tide conditions. You can rent your equipment at the inn as well.

After your morning row, head to the village of **Mendocino**. Atop the weather-beaten bluffs is a collection of vintage Victorian buildings that create a storybook silhouette against the often foggy horizon.

Main Street is filled with relics from the booming logging era. Every few steps is something worth noting, including the **Ford House Museum**, built in 1861 and paying homage to one of the town's founding families. Nearby is the redwood-built **Presbyterian Church** (*photo at right*) with its striking steeple dating back to the 1860s, the 1866 **Masonic Temple**, and the re- markable **Mendocino Hotel and Gardens Suites** teetering at the edge of the street. Sandwiched in between you'll find the **Mendocino Art Center** show-  casing works from local talent and the adorable **Gallery Bookshop** for children. As for art galleries, there are plenty within the village.

After you've spent the rest of the afternoon strolling through town, poking your head in shops, and admiring local art, take a stroll along the jagged headlands or, from near the church, follow the stairs that trail down to the beach. This is an ideal vantage point to watch the sunset.

Before bidding farewell to your Mendocino weekend, stop into the classic **Mendocino Hotel and Garden Suites** to do a little wine tasting. The wine list is updated quarterly and features selections from both well-known California wineries as well as local bou- tique vineyards. Even more intoxicating than the wine list itself is the setting in which to enjoy your syrah, pinot noir or chardonnay. Listen to the faint sound of foghorns as you cozy up to the centuries-old Dutch fireplace. What a great way to toast your fantastic weekend in Mendocino. *Info*: www.mendocinohotel.com. Tel. 707/937-0511. 45080 Main Street.

A WONDERFUL WEEK ON THE NORTH COAST

The beauty of the North Coast, from **Eureka** to **Mendocino** and a little beyond, is something that must be experienced. Your days will be fulfilling but never frenzied as you scour the pristine coastline, visit historic towns, and stand in the shadow of the **ancient redwood groves** dating back several hundred years. When someone utters the phrase "to get away from it all," the North Coast is surely what they must have in mind.

RECOMMENDED PLAN: A week along the North Coast will leave you feeling rested and energized. You'll spend three nights in Ferndale, three nights in Mendocino with a final night spent in Muir Beach, which makes it easy to catch your flight from either San Francisco or Oakland Airports. You'll want to follow my *One Great Day* and *Fantastic Weekend* itineraries that cover both Ferndale's highlights, as well as the charms of Mendocino, adding **The Redwood Coast** and **Anderson Valley** to your itinerary plus a few other unexpected destinations as well.

The North Coast is not the easiest place to reach. If you start in Ferndale, which is what I recommend because you then move south to Mendocino, it's a five hour drive from San Francisco Airport. The scenery is spectacular, but you need to factor in the time to get here when planning your trip. The main route is Highway 101, which parallels the Pacific Ocean. The **Eureka/ Arcata Airport** (ACV), located about an hour north of Ferndale, is served by two carriers, United

Express and Alaska/Horizon Air. Both have daily flights from San Francisco, Sacramento, Los Angeles and Portland.

The Redwood Coast
You'll spend your nights in Ferndale at one of the recommended inns in the *Best Sleeps & Eats* chapter while exploring the fascinating haunts of the Redwood Coast. As you venture north on Highway 101 towards Humboldt County, be sure to stop at one of the Drive-Thru Trees. The **Chandelier Tree** in Leggett and the **Shrine Drive-Thru Tree** in Myers Flat (*see photo below*) are both located

off Highway 101. These soaring giants serve as mini tunnels allowing you to maneuver your vehicle through their trunk. Shrine Tree also has a step-thru stump and a drive-on tree, which is a giant trunk that has fallen and now has a partially paved ramp.

Continuing north, you'll take the majestic **Avenue of the Giants** scenic drive which begins just north of Garberville. The 31-mile portion of Highway 101 boasts the most magnificent display of redwoods and, along the way, you'll find plenty of conveniences. **Humboldt Redwoods State Park,** which has the largest remaining stand of virgin redwoods in the world, cradles the shady avenue. If you like kitschy gifts shops and tacky treasures, you'll find the lion's share as you travel along the **Avenue of the Giants**. There is everything from eau de redwood perfume to chunky redwood clocks. A few artisans are found here as well, including glass blowers and carvers.

Trinidad, Fern Canyon & Redwood National Forest

Take a day to spend roaming the region. From Ferndale, head north on Highway 101 stopping in the coastal town of Trinidad, the smallest, oldest and most westerly city in the state, for a relaxing walk along **Trinidad State Beach**. Located about 19 miles north of Eureka, this patch of paradise is tucked in a secluded cove near town. You'll hike through the woods, across open bluffs, atop headlands filled with wildflowers before wandering down to the shoreline. Low tide is the most enjoyable time and there is a natural arch near the north end.

A great place to spot grey whales on their migration is from Trinidad Head. The **Trinidad Memorial Lighthouse**, a replica of the original 1871 beacon built in 1949, is located here as well.

From Trinidad, drive a few miles north of Orick along Highway 101. Exit Davidson Road and turn left. You'll continue through **Elk Meadow** and off of the paved road. For the next six miles you'll enjoy one of the most spectacular scenic drives as you motor onward to **Gold Bluffs Beach**, whose name comes from the gold dust that was mined here decades ago. Here you'll find **Fern Canyon**, a narrow and moist gorge cloaked from one end to the other in ferns and moss. The area has abundant wildlife, so you're apt to spot elk, deer and maybe a raccoon or two.

Next, head to the Redwood Groves found inside **Redwood National Park** on Highway 101 where the majestic trees create an eerie twilight effect even on the sunniest of days. The **Ladybird Johnson Grove**, named for the former first lady and naturalist, is located on **Bald Hill Road** just a mile or so north of Orick along Highway 101. You can also embark on a ranger-led program or hike June to Labor Day. *Info*: Tel. 707/464-6101 to arrange a guided tour.

Eureka

The town of **Eureka** is about an hour from Ferndale and is bordered on one side by Humboldt Bay and on the other by the lush giant redwoods. Its architectural treasures hail from the Victorian era as well, and Eureka ranks among the top small arts communities in America, too.

Eureka, like Ferndale, was overlooked during the urban development of the 1960s. The old commercial center, established around 1850, remains intact. Although Eureka is thought of as a lumber town, it was first developed as a transportation and supply center for the Gold Rush taking place along the Klamath and Trinity Rivers. As a result, a waterfront business district emerged with offices, shops and saloons; it remains the pulse of the city today. **Old Town** is filled with great vintage buildings now operating as bookstores, coffeehouses, art galleries, and restaurants.

At the intersection of M and 2nd Streets is the former home of Lumber Barron William Carson. **Carson Mansion**, built in 1884, is a twist of turrets and towers punctu-

Historic Lighthouses

Northern California has some **spectacular lighthouses** along the coast and many offer tours. Most were established during the mid 19th to the early 20th centuries. Some have been completely restored, while others are just a shell of their former selves. The following lighthouses are listed from north to south:

- **Crescent City Lighthouse** (*photo below*), Crescent City
- **St. George Reef Lighthouse**, near Crescent City
- **Trinidad Head Lighthouse**, Trinidad
- **Humboldt Bay Lighthouse**, Humboldt Bay
- **Cape Mendocino Lighthouse**, Shelter Cove
- **Punta Gorda Lighthouse**, near Petrolia
- **Point Cabrillo Lighthouse**, Point Cabrillo
- **Point Arena Lighthouse**, Point Arena
- **Point Reyes Lighthouse**, Point Reyes

ated with columned porches, numerous gables, and ornate gingerbread detail. If any one building defines the Victorian era, it's the Carson Mansion. The home remained in the Carson family until 1950, before it was sold to a private club. Tours of the interiors are not available, but you can view and photograph the mansion located at 143 M Street.

Eureka's Colorful Art

Eureka's fledgling **artists' community** is evident at every turn. Many of the buildings' exteriors serve as colorful canvases and are part of the town's **mural program**. A self-guided tour spotlights the many magnificent works that depict Eureka's history and sense of humor. Most of the murals are located in Old Town. *Info:* Tel. 800/346-3482.

After cruising around downtown, cruise Humboldt Bay aboard the *Madaket.* One of the last surviving, original ferries used to transport mill workers and their families around the bay, the vessel is the nation's oldest continuous ferry in service. Built in 1910, the *Madaket* saw its demise in 1972 when the completion of a local bridge put it out of business. It was finally restored in 1989 and given a new lease on life. This vintage vessel, which holds up to 45 people, takes passengers on a 75-minute cruise along the Eureka waterfront. Points of interest include the discoveries of Humboldt Bay, the history of the timber industry, wildlife, maritime tales and some Native American history as well. Cruises are seasonal and offered Tuesday-Sunday from June to September and weekends only May and October. *Info*: www.humboldtmaritimemuseum.com. Tel. 707/445-1910. Foot of F Street. Adults $15, children $7.50.

If you arrive in Eureka in the off-season when the *Madaket* isn't running, you can still get a taste of history by dining at the **Samoa Cookhouse**. Opened in 1890 as a lumber camp-style restaurant known then as the Hammond Lumber Company Cookhouse, it was the hub, community center and kitchen for loggers. "Come and get it" was a familiar cry, and when the whistle blew to signal the end of the work day, the men were more than eager to sit down to a big, family-style meal. Today, the restaurant is a popular destination with locals and is open for breakfast, lunch and dinner seven days a week. Check out the restaurant's logging museum. *Info*: www.samoacookhouse.com. Tel. 707/442-1659. Samoa, 511 Vance Avenue.

Ferndale to Mendocino
Upon leaving Ferndale, head south on Highway 101. Near Leggett, you'll turn off and head towards Highway 1. Take Highway 1 south to Mendocino. Most of my hotel recommendations are located south of Mendocino village, except for The Mendocino Inn and Garden Suites which is located in the village.

You'll want to follow the weekend itinerary outlined earlier in this chapter, as well as explore some other destinations near Mendocino that are equally interesting, including:

Anderson Valley
Pity the poor traveler who doesn't take the time to stop and smell the grapes while passing through Anderson Valley. **Highway 128**, which cuts a twisted swathe through the leafy appellation, is just a means to an end for many motorists as they race towards the Mendocino Coast from Highway 101. Ah, but that just  leaves the rest of us with more wines to taste. Before you venture into a tasting room, you'll want to know a few things about wine tasting etiquette:

* At the tasting bar, a host/hostess will greet you and explain the wines available for tasting and let you know if there is a fee to taste.
* When tasting, whites are presented first followed by reds. Dessert wines are last.

- Be sure to savor the wines you taste.
- Don't feel as if you need to drink all the wines available. If you just want to taste reds or prefer only whites, let your host/hostess know.
- Don't feel pressured to drink all the wine in your glass. That's what the dump bucket is for.
- Typically, you only ask to taste a wine again if you're interested in purchasing a bottle.
- Cleanse your palette with each glass. Usually water or crackers are available at the tasting bar.
- When a fee is charged, it's perfectly acceptable for two people to share a glass and pay only a single tasting fee.

The region is ripe for wine growing. Blankets of evening fog create moderate temperatures allowing grapes, like the fragile pinot noir, to thrive. Chardonnay, White Riesling and gewürztraminer also do well in the cool coastal climate. Motor along Highway 128 through the quirky named towns of Boonville and Philo, stopping here and there to sample the varietals. Tasting rooms run the gamut from picnic tables scattered around backyard wineries to state-of-the-art tasting rooms boasting vineyard vistas. If you don't fancy yourself an oenophile, then there are other destinations to explore. The **Anderson Valley Brewing Company** offers tours of its Bavarian-style brewery which turns out stellar ports, stouts and ales. They also have a beer garden and a tasting room. *Info*: www.avcb.com. Tel. 707/895-2337. Booneville, 17700 Highway 253.

You Harpin' Boontling?

Boontling, local slang, was created by Alexander Valley residents in 1880 for their own amusement and to guard against nosey outsiders. For a time, Boontling became the primary language for many residents with some having difficulty reverting back to proper English when needed. A few terms you may hear in these parts:

- **Harpin'** means talking
- **Shark** means to stump
- **Bahl Hornin'** equates to good drinking
- **Baldies** are the grassy hills east of Boonville
- **Briney** means ocean
- **Frattey** is wine
- **Shoveltooth** is a doctor

The all-organic **Philo Apple Farm** boasts a bounty of fruit, chutney, jams and jellies all grown on the surrounding 35 acres. It also offers four orchard cottages for overnight stays. From February to November the farm conducts cooking classes most every weekend. Keep in mind these classes are filled 6-12 months in advance, so plan accordingly. The price includes cottage accommodations, all meals, **cooking classes**, and wine. Menus vary with the seasons, what's sprouting in the garden, and group demographics. You'll walk away with inspirational recipes, some new and timesaving techniques, and a full tummy as you eat what you create. On a final note, the owners of the Philo Apple Farm are the former proprietors of the highly-acclaimed French Laundry in Yountville (Napa) now owned by Celebrity Chef Thomas Keller. *Info*: www.philoapplefarm.com. Tel. 707/895-2333. Philo, 18501 Greenwood Road.

Downtown Boonville also has a smattering of shops and restaurants, including the **Farmhouse Mercantile**, offering interesting items for the home. The **Boonville Hotel**, along Highway 128, is also an interesting stop. This modern roadhouse offers stylish rooms, a fabulous restaurant, and a wine bar.

Willits

Like many of the towns along the North Coast, there isn't much to them. Willits, a small rural community established in the 1800s, is one of them. But what puts Willits on the map, especially in recent years with the release of a book and

Anderson Valley Wineries

Anderson Valley is home to some great boutique wineries as well as some well-known vintners, too. Do a little sipping in Philo at:

• **Navarro Vineyards** – great views and picnic spots
• **Lazy Creek** – hidden locale with palatable pinot noir
• **Roederer Estate** – sensational sparkling wines and a fabulous tasting room
• **Husch** – inexpensive vintages wines and an intimate tasting room

a feature film, is a horse named **Seabiscuit**. Owned by Charles Howard, trained by Tom Smith, and ridden by Red Pollard, Seabiscuit made horseracing history. When he retired in 1940,

Seabiscuit spent his final years at Howard's **Ridgewood Ranch** in Willits. A statue of Seabiscuit was finally unveiled at the ranch in June 2007. Docent-led walking tours of the ranch include a visit to Seabiscuit's modest barn, which is especially significant since his is the only one that still exists from that era. Other barns from horseracing's glory days, such as the one that belonged to Seabiscuit's rival, War Admiral, and his great grandsire, the legendary Man O War, were destroyed when Glenn Riddle Farm was developed. You'll also see the mare barn, the historic craftsman home of Charles Howard, hear anecdotes, and receive a commemorative souvenir. *Info*: www.seabiscuitheritage.org Tel. 707/459-5992. Willits. Adults $15; children 11 and under free. Call for tour dates and times.

Mendocino to Muir Beach
There are a few **driving options** from Mendocino to Muir Beach. The slower and more scenic route, not to mention treacherous, is to take Highway 1 the entire way. A compromise, which combines both scenic and sensible routes, is to cut over to Highway 101 near Bodega Bay. The final and quickest option is to just take Highway 128 through Anderson Valley to Highway 101 and head south. It's not nearly as scenic, but you'll arrive much faster. Spend your last night at the lovely and remote **Pelican Bay Inn** in Muir Beach. Seemingly plucked from the English countryside, this seven room hideaway is close enough to catch an afternoon flight from San Francisco or Oakland Airports, but remarkably isolated. The inn's pub is highly acclaimed and has a strictly British menu. *Info*: www.pelicaninn.com. Tel. 415/383-6000. Muir Beach. 10 Pacific Way.

If you arrive early, you can explore the **Tomales Bay Region**, which includes the towns of Iverness, Muir Beach, Olema, Marshall, Point Reyes (*photo at left*), Stinson Beach, and Tomales. Just ramble along **Highway 1**, which is the common thread connecting these tiny hamlets together. Blink and you're likely to miss a town altogether. **Point Reyes** is home to a collection of culinary offerings including **Cowgirl Creamery,** which began nine years ago in a renovated barn, where you can watch the artisan cheeses being made or sip wine at the Cowgirl Cantina. There is also **Point Reyes Vineyards,** owned and farmed by the same family for three generations. Tastings take place on weekends from 9am-5pm.

Nearby **Marshall** is home to the **Hog Island Oyster Company** (*see photo below*), which has the Martha Stewart stamp of approval, and **Tomales Bay Oyster Company,** the state's oldest continuously-run shellfish farm. Both welcome visitors and offer picnic areas. Hog Island takes it a bit further allowing visitors to shuck their own oysters, douse them in the farm's trademark **Hog Wash,** and then grill them. Hog Island requires picnic reservations, Tomales Bay does not. *Info*: Tel. 415/663-9218 for Hog Island; Tel. 415/663-1242 for Tomales Bay.

If you decide to travel Highway 1 the entire way from Mendocino to Muir Beach, you'll pass through the places mentioned above. Start out early and stop at those that interest you, then check into the Pelican Inn for the night and get a good rest. Traveling along Highway 1 will take up much of the day, especially when you factor in a few stops. Make sure you depart Mendocino early so you can arrive at Muir Beach before sunset. It's not advised to drive along Highway 1 after dark.

Muir Beach, The Pelican Inn, oyster shucking, and a beautiful coastal drive: what better way to end an unbelievable week along the North Coast?

8. NORTHERN CALIFORNIA IN TWO WEEKS

This two-week suggested itinerary will allow you to explore Northern California and all its wonders at a leisurely pace, giving you plenty of opportunity to take in the scenery and savor life's simple pleasures.

Not only will you visit the major metropolises, **San Francisco** and **San Jose**, you'll also experience the undeniable beauty of the **Central** and **North Coasts**, the premier winegrowing region of **Napa** and **Sonoma Counties**, and the divine destinations of **Yosemite National Park** and **Lake Tahoe** found in the **High Sierra**. Of course, there are some unexpected stops along the way. No matter where the road takes you, it will be one that is less traveled. You won't just be another visitor to Northern California; instead, you'll be a passionate participant eager to plot your own course and free to experience the best the region has to offer.

RECOMMENDED PLAN: Most people flying to Northern California may assume that San Francisco International Airport (SFO) is the logical choice for arrival, but **San Jose International Airport (SJC) might be a better alternative.** SJC is less crowded and, for this two-week itinerary, a better selection because it's closer to the Central Coast, which is your final destination. If you have an afternoon or evening return flight, you can always eliminate San Jose and add another night to your itinerary elsewhere. Other airport options include San Francisco International and Oakland International, the latter is actually an easier commute to the city than the former.

The agenda I've created allows you to spend **three days in San Francisco, a day in Yosemite, two days in Lake Tahoe, two days in the Wine Country, two days along the North Coast, and two days in Carmel on the Central Coast.** Your last evening will be spent in San Jose, which will put you close to the airport for your return trip home. I've planned it so that travel between destinations take four hours or less by car. On travel days, I suggest you get an early start so that you arrive at your next destination by early afternoon.

Tip: If you fly into San Jose International Airport, don't take congested Highway 101 into San Francisco. Instead, take the road less traveled – Interstate 280 – an eight-lane highway that travels along the San Francisco peninsula.

SAN FRANCISCO
San Francisco seems like several small towns woven

into one large metropolis. There are so many fun and fabulous neighborhoods each with their own flair and personality. Every block brings with it a new adventure, from historic landmarks to haute cuisine. San Francisco constantly ranks among the nation's top travel destinations, and it's a great place to kick off your Northern California road trip. You'll spend three days in the City by the Bay, which should give you ample time to explore **Union Square, Chinatown, The Embarcadero, North Beach, Cow Hollow and The Marina**.

In Town
Chances are your hotel is on or near Union Square, which is abuzz with a flurry of shoppers, visitors and those just passing through as they make their way to other parts of the city.

You'll begin your trip here at the corner of **Powell and Geary** near the historic Westin St. Francis Hotel. The square, named for a series of violent pro-union mass demonstrations that took place on the land the night before the start of the Civil War, is now a shopping mecca. Look around, and decide which stores appeal to you: Macy's, Neiman Marcus, Williams-Sonoma, Tiffany & Co, or any of the other dozens of shops that line the square and adjoining avenues. The cable cars, which move along Powell Street, originate from the cable car turnaround just three blocks down at Market Street.

Eventually, make your way to the opposite side of the square to **Stockton Street** where vintage iron gates are propped open to reveal the tiny alleyway of **Maiden Lane**. The narrow breezeway, which ends a short distance at Kearney Street, is a pedestrian-only shopping destination. At **140 Maiden Lane** is the only Frank Lloyd Wright building within city limits.

Chinatown
Halfway down Maiden Lane is **Grant Avenue**. This street leads up to **Chinatown**, the largest and oldest Chinatown outside of Asia. In 1948, the first Chinese immigrants arrived to the city – two men and a woman. The entrance to this authentic and historic district is marked with an imposing **dragon gate** at Grant Avenue and Bush Street. Swaying above Chinatown's streets are

paper lanterns and below are dragon-entwined lampposts. You'll also notice that street signs are written in both English and Chinese.

As you wander down **Grant Avenue**, you'll pass by a number of shops displaying Cheongsam dresses, mahjong tiles, silk pajamas, hand-carved chopsticks, and many other items. Between Jackson and Washington Streets is Ross Alley where the **Golden Gate Fortune Cookie Company** is located at No. 52. Opened in 1962, it is the only fortune cookie company left in Chinatown, and visitors can watch the crescent-shaped cookies being made. **Hang Ah Tea Room** at 1 Pagoda Place is tucked away at the end of a small alley and is one of Chinatown's oldest dim sum eateries.

The Embarcadero
Make your way back down Grant Avenue towards Union Square, which will end at **Market Street**. If you look right you can catch a glimpse of Nordstrom and a galleria of shops tucked behind glass

Don't Miss in Chinatown...

Amazing architecture and landmarks not to be missed:

• **Chinese Telephone Company**, 743 Washington Boulevard (now the Bank of Canton)
• **Sing Chong Building**, near the intersection of California and Grant
• **First Chinese Baptist Church**, 15 Waverly Place
• **Old St. Mary's**, 660 California Street
• **Golden Gate Fortune Cookie Company**, 52 Ross Alley
• **Hang Ah Tea Room**, 1 Pagoda Place
• **Dragon Gate**, Grant Avenue and Bush Street

doors. The cable car turn-around is also located here. If you head left, you can walk down Market Street through the **Financial District**. At the end of Market Street, which is maybe a 20-30 minute walk, is the **Ferry Building Marketplace**.

Built in 1898 on the site of the 1875 Ferry House, the building emerged a transportation hub for anyone arriving via train from the east, as well as the workforce who commuted daily from the East Bay and Marin County. From the start of the Gold Rush until the 1930s, before the opening of the Golden Gate and Bay Bridges, ferryboat was the only mode of transportation to the city unless you were arriving from the peninsula. By the 1950s, the building was used very little until it received a new lease on life a few years ago with an extensive preservation and restoration effort. The transformation yielded a vibrant public food hall with high-end culinary retailers, a cache of restaurants, and a bi-weekly farmers market. Charming stalls carry everything from organic mushrooms to fresh-plucked oysters to hand-pressed olive oils and artisan cheeses. You can nibble your way through the cavernous building or sit down inside one of the many restaurants, including the famed **Slanted Door.**

> ### Ferry Marketplace Tours
>
> **San Francisco City Guides** offer free walking tours of the historic **Ferry Building Marketplace** every Saturday, Sunday and Tuesday starting at noon. You can also sample fresh foods and produce from local farms. The Ferry Plaza Farmers Market will be underway, too. *Info*: www.sfcityguides.org.

After poking around the Ferry Building Marketplace, walk out the front door and turn right. Follow the sidewalk along the waterfront, also known as The Embarcadero. You can also try to catch the **F-Line**, the historic streetcars that travel down Embarcadero Center. The vintage vehicles, pulled from the streets of Boston, Chicago and Milan, are painted in their original colors.

The Embarcadero has a rich and bawdy history that dates back to the Gold Rush era when it was known as the Barbary Coast. In 1849, some 700 vessels made their way here during an eight-month span with thousands of fortune seekers on board hoping to find gold during the frenzy. After becoming beached in their berths, some ships were cleverly converted to warehouses and saloons.

Continue along the Embarcadero until you reach **Pier 33** near the intersection of Bay Street. This is where you can purchase tickets to **Alcatraz Island** and, when it's time, you'll catch the ferry from here, too. Tickets must be purchased in advance, so do this as soon as possible; especially if you're traveling on weekends or during the summer months. The nighttime tours are a bit more interesting and eerie than the daytime tours, but both are very informative, interesting and not in the least bit touristy. A tour of "The Rock," which lasts 2 1/2 to 3 hours, is a self-guided audio tour that takes you from the rocky dock to the cellhouse level. You'll learn of infamous events, such as escape attempts and food riots, as well as time spent in solitary confinement. Many of the narrators on the audio tour are former prison guards and prisoners.

As you walk from Pier 33 towards Pier 39, the scenery changes from waterfront warehouses to legions of shops, fish grottos and scattered street performers. Pier 39 is extremely touristy, but it's worth walking to the end for a photo of Alcatraz Island in the background or the throngs of seals that lounge on the docks to the left.

When you leave Pier 39, continue along **Fisherman's Wharf** where you'll encounter some talented—and not so talented—

> **ALTERNATIVE PLAN**
>
> An alternative to Alcatraz Island is **Angel Island**, often referred to as the "Ellis Island of the West." You'll catch the **Blue and Gold Fleet** ferry just a few docks down from Pier 33 at Pier 39, which is an outdoor shopping and entertainment complex where you can also watch the lazy seals lounge on the docks and ride the double-decker carousel. The ferry will take you to the middle of the bay where the 740-acre island is located. A guided tour illustrates Angel Island's rich history as a Civil War encampment, a quarantine station, a POW camp, a missile base, and an immigration station where 250,000 Chinese immigrants were processed with an average detention of two weeks.

street performers. You'll be expected to drop some change in their bucket if you pose for a picture, snap their picture, or stay long enough to watch their act. Not doing so may result in a few minutes of public humiliation. You'll notice a cluster of stalls near the waterfront selling fresh fish, crab, and other take and carry items. **Boudin's Bakery and Café**, known for their incredible sourdough bread, is along this stretch, too. You can pick up tasty sandwiches in the downstairs bakery or enjoy a sit-down meal (okay for kids, too) upstairs in the restaurant. Boudin's also has a culinary shop where you'll find a nice selection of gadgets and gifts. You can grab a cup of coffee at Peet's, which is located here, too.

You probably haven't noticed, but the street has become Jefferson. Continue along Jefferson and turn up Hyde Street. Off to your right is the Cable Car turnaround headed for Union Square. Across from the turnaround is the **Buena Vista**, where the Irish Coffee was invented. Go inside to look around or belly up to the bar for a little pick me up before moving on.

Ghirardelli Square

Outside the Buena Vista, you'll see **Ghirardelli Square** to your left in the distance. You might want to poke through the collection of shops and eateries, including **Ghirardelli Chocolate** where you can sit down for an ice cream sundae, milkshake, banana split and other concoctions.

North Beach & Beyond
Now head up **Hyde Street** (it's a steep couple of blocks) **to Bay Street**. Take a left on Bay Street and continue until you reach Columbus where you'll turn right. Continue along Columbus Avenue into the heart of **North Beach**, the Italian neighborhood.

Or, you can catch the cable car across the street from the Buena Vista at the turnaround. Just to warn you, there is usually a long line and sometimes the wait can be up to an hour on weekends. Take the cable car to the top of the hill and get

off at Lombard Street in the Russian Hill neighborhood. From here, you can walk down the "crookedest street" in the world to reach North Beach. Lombard eventually intersects with Columbus Avenue.

After passing several espresso shops, trattorias, and bakeries displaying fresh canolli you'll realize you have arrived at North Beach. At 261 Columbus Avenue is **City Lights Bookstore**, a favorite gathering place for **Jack Kerouac** and other writers from the Beat Generation. Alongside the bookstore is Jack Kerouac Alley. Nearby, at **666 Filbert Street**, is St. Peter and Paul Catholic Church where **Joe DiMaggio** received his first communion as a young boy, married his first wife in 1939, and was eulogized in 1999. He and **Marilyn Monroe** were married at City Hall in 1954, but their wedding photos were taken on the steps of the church.

Don't Miss ...

- An evening tour of **Alcatraz Island**
- A stroll through the **Ferry Building Marketplace**
- The chance to dangle from the side of a **cable car**
- The throngs of **sunning sea lions** at Fisherman's Wharf
- A walk down crooked **Lombard Street**
- Lunching at **The Rotunda** inside Neiman Marcus at Union Square
- A walk (or drive) across the **Golden Gate Bridge**
- Having an Irish Coffee at the **Buena Vista** near Fisherman's Wharf.
- A visit to the **Japanese Tea Garden** in Golden Gate Park

After wandering around North Beach, walk back down Columbus Avenue to **Union Street**. At the south corner of Union and Columbus in front of the park, hop on **Bus #45** marked Lyon & Greenwich. You'll take the bus for about 15 minutes until you reach Gough Street, where you'll exit. This is the start of **Cow Hollow.**

Union Street is an out-of-the-way shopping district frequented mostly by locals. Art galleries, sidewalk cafes and one-of-a-kind retailers are housed inside original Victorian structures. This is a fun area to explore with shopping opportunities located on both sides of the street. Once you've had some time to browse around, make your way down to **The Marina** on foot by taking **Fillmore Street**. It's an easy downhill walk that will maybe take you 20 minutes or less. Once you reach **Chestnut Street**, you've arrived. This is another neighborhood filled with an interesting mix of shops, restaurants and coffee houses. The **Lucca Delicatessen** at 2120 Chestnut Street is a great place to pick up an ample-sized sandwich to enjoy now or later. **Books, Inc.** at 2251 Chestnut is one of the city's independent booksellers stocking classics and bestsellers and features with an extensive children's section.

Tired of shopping? Walk from Union Street down Laguna Street to Chestnut. At the southwest corner of this intersection, catch Bus #28/Daly City to **Golden Gate Park**. You'll exit at Park Presidio Boulevard and Fulton Street. From here, you can walk through the park, which is larger than New York City's Central Park. The nearest attraction from your bus stop is the **Rose Garden** off John F. Kennedy Drive. Or ask your bus driver for a transfer and catch Bus #5/Trans Bay Terminal at the southwest corner of Fulton and Park Presidio and exit at 12th Avenue. From here you can walk to the **Japanese Tea Garden,** one of the city's most serene spots since 1894.

HIGH SIERRA: YOSEMITE & LAKE TAHOE

It's back to nature in the High Sierra region of Northern California. From the sheer cliffs and rock formations of Yosemite National Park to the sheer snow-covered ski runs that Lake Tahoe is famous for, both destinations are a breath of fresh air. Your visit to Yosemite will be brief but fulfilling. With two days in Lake Tahoe, you'll get to enjoy many of the area's highlights.

San Francisco to Yosemite

Make your way from San Francisco to **Yosemite National Park** heading east on the Bay Bridge. Although many people enter the park through Merced on Highway 140, you're going to enter through Oakhurst on Highway 41 to begin your scenic drive through the park. While en route from the city through Central California, cityscapes are replaced by rambling ranches, grazing cattle, and modern windmills that generate electric power. You'll pass through **Modesto**, the city of "water, wealth, contentment, health" and birthplace of director **George Lucas.** His hometown was inspiration for the classic film *American Graffiti*. If you happen to be passing by during the month of June, the town pulls out its poodle skirts and hula hoops for its **Graffiti Summer**.

Yosemite National Park

As you enter the park on Highway 41 through Mariposa and Oakhurst (if you're staying in Oakhurst, go ahead and check into your hotel then begin the drive into the park), you'll travel through Wawona to **Tunnel View**. Once you exit the tunnel, you'll see a beautiful panorama. There are two parking areas, go ahead and stop if you feel inclined or continue onward into the Valley where your next stop is **Bridalveil Fall**. Here you'll witness spectacular views of both the famed **El Capitan** and the falls themselves.

Staying at Yosemite

Everyone wants to stay at **The Ahwahnee**, but if you don't book months in advance getting a room may be more difficult than you think. There are some other great lodging choices within the park, including **Yosemite Lodge at the Falls** and the **Wawona Hotel**. You can also find cabins and tented cabins for a more authentic "roughing it" experience at **Curry Village, Housekeeping Camp, Tuolumne Meadows Lodge, White Wolf Lodge,** and **Yosemite High Sierra Camps**. *Info*: www.yosemitepark.com.

In the heart of the Valley, park at one of the day-use lots and board the free shuttle bus to the **Valley Visitor Center** in **Yosemite Village**. Here you can visit the **Ansel Adams** and **Yosemite Museums** where ongoing demonstrations and a reconstructed Indian Village of Ahwahnee are found behind the museum. The **Yosemite Cemetery** is located across the street and is the final resting place for many Native Americans. From here, board the free shuttle which ferries you around the valley floor. It's a continuous one-hour loop, but you have the option to exit at places of interest, including Lower Yosemite Falls, Nature Center at Happy Isles, the historic Ahwahnee Hotel or Sentinel Bridge, which boasts spectacular vistas of Half Dome. Finally, check into your lodge for the night and check out the star-strewn sky above.

From Yosemite to Lake Tahoe
Take Highway 120 from Yosemite to Highway 49 towards Lake Tahoe. Sometimes referred to as the **Gold Rush Trail**, you'll motor through the state's mother lode towns. The road twists and turns as it makes its way past meadows, lakes and rivers. **Sutter Creek**, the halfway point between Yosemite and Lake Tahoe, is one of the many towns worth making a quick stop.

Begin your time in Tahoe at **Emerald Bay State Park**, a National Natural Landmark and home to **Vikingsholm**. This once private estate, one of the best examples of Scandinavian architecture in the western hemisphere, is located on Fannette Island, the only isle in all of Lake Tahoe. If you scuba dive, explore Emerald Bay's underwater park where many abandoned vessels, some used during the construction of Vikingsholm, lend themselves well to watery exploration.

Emerald Bay State Park is ideal to visit when it's warm, but if you're here in the winter why not hit the slopes? Plan on using an entire day (two if you're a real enthusiast) at one of the area's many resorts, including **Alpine Meadows, Heavenly Ski Resort** or **Squaw Valley USA**, just to name a few, where you can ski or snowboard. Not a skier, but still enjoy the snow? There's snowshoeing, dog-sledding, sleigh rides, ice skating, and sledding.

Next, freshen up at your hotel before heading out for the evening. One of the most amazing sites is **the viewing platform at Heavenly Resort**. You'll need to arrive by 4pm to board the eight-passenger, glass enclosed gondola. The nearly 2 1/2 mile trip takes you to the viewing platform several feet above where you can watch the sunset and enjoy the incredible views.

After the sun slips behind the mountains, drive over to Crystal Bay where the infamous **Cal-Neva Resort** stands. Once owned by Frank Sinatra, the resort hosts **walking tours** on Friday and Saturday evenings at 7pm. You'll visit Marilyn Monroe's cabin, clandestine tunnels, and other areas not open to the public. You can also poke around and create your own self-guided tour if you happen to be here on another evening. Cal-Neva's **Circle Bar** is a nice place to unwind beneath the prism dome before — or after — spending a few hours in the casino.

THE WINE COUNTRY: NAPA & SONOMA COUNTIES
With two days allotted in The Wine Country, you'll never be at a loss to tantalize your taste buds with artisan cheeses, plump olives and fresh-pressed olive oil. Then, of course, there are the

tasting rooms themselves where you can sample wonderful whites, robust reds, chardonnay or cabernet – take your pick. There is also time to take in one of the region's historic sites and, perhaps, a warm mud bath, too.

From Lake Tahoe to The Wine Country
You'll take Highway 50, which runs coast to coast, passing through **Sacramento**. It's about a 3 1/2 hour drive from Lake Tahoe to The Wine Country, so you may want to stop at the state's capital city and maybe visit the Historic District at 2nd and K Streets. You'll continue on Highway 50 to Highway 80 East as you make your way to Highway 12, which leads to The Wine Country.

Make your way to Sonoma's Historic Plaza, which is steeped in history. Just read the various plaques as you make your way through the square. There are also some fabulous finds for shoppers along the plaza, including home décor, original artwork, and culinary keepsakes. You might want to visit the **Mission San Francisco Solano** at the corner of Spain and 1st Streets. It's was the last to be built in the 21-mission chain. Next, hop in the car and head north on Highway 29 towards the town of Napa where you'll spend a few hours at **COPIA: The American Center for Food, Wine & the Arts**. This non-profit culinary center is where you can do some wine tasting, food sampling, traipse through organic gardens, and peruse the art exhibits.

Continue north on Highway 29 stopping at some of the tasting rooms en route: **Turnbull Wine Cellars, Supery Vineyards, St. Clements Vineyards**. Pick up some sandwiches at **Oakville Grocery** in Rutherford, purchase a bottle of wine at some tasting room, and enjoy a picnic lunch among the vineyards. When you reach **St. Helena**, pull the car over and wander along Main Street (also Highway 29) poking around the high-end stores and boutiques.

Once back in the car, continue along Highway 29 to the **Culinary Institute of America's West Coast campus**, a learning center for those interested in the fields of food, wine, health and hospitality. Tours are offered on select days for just $5 per person or you can just wander around the school's culinary shop or dine at the school's restaurant. Further up on Highway 29 is the spa town of **Calistoga**. Lincoln Avenue, as well as neighboring streets, is lined with spas boasting natural hot springs, baths of mud, and several styles of massage. Pay a visit to Calistoga's **Old Faithful Geyser**, one of only three in the entire world erupting on cue every 20-30 minutes.

ALTERNATIVE PLAN
If you're only interested in learning about the region's selection of wines, there are many tasting rooms along Highway 29. You can also motor along the **Silverado Trail**, from Napa to St. Helena and beyond. This less traveled highway is brimming with vineyards, tasting rooms, and places to picnic.

Next, take a scenic drive towards the coast and through the redwoods. From Calistoga, take Highway 128 passing through more wine country villages until you reach Highway 101. Go south on Highway 101 exiting at Highway 12 in Santa Rosa. Head west through Sonoma County, past **Sebastopol** and **Bodega** before the road ends at **Bodega Bay** and Highway 1. From Bodega Bay, head north up Highway 1 towards Jenner veering onto Route116-Sonoma County Scenic Byway as you near Jenner.

Along this route you'll find some delightful tasting rooms as you pass the towns of Duncan Mills, Monte Rio and Guerneville. Just outside of Guerneville is the **Korbel Champagne Cellars**, which offers a 50-minute **Champagne Cellars Tour** departing every 45 minutes from 10am to 3pm daily. Return to Route 116, where you'll come upon **Sebastopol**, another wonderful wine country town where you can do more shopping.

THE NORTH COAST: MENDOCINO

Tucked away along the windswept coast is this tiny New England-style village brimming with shops and galleries. Two days will give you enough time to enjoy a vintage train ride, do some wine tasting in the **Anderson Valley**, and kayak along the Big River.

Unfortunately, there just isn't enough time to visit both Ferndale and Mendocino. You'll spend most of your time driving instead of enjoying the destinations. I recommend Mendocino because it's closer to both the Wine Country and your next destination, the Central Coast, which will result less driving time.

From The Wine Country to Mendocino

Take Highway 101 North to Highway 128, which will take you through the Anderson Valley. While en route to Mendocino, stop in the towns of **Boonville** and **Philo,** visit the wineries, do a little sampling, and enjoy the bucolic scenery as you make your way towards Mendocino.

You've spent your first day wine tasting, now use your second day to travel the rails aboard the **Skunk Train**, which has been hailed as one of the 10 most scenic rail trips in North America. You'll board the historic train north of Mendocino in **Fort Bragg** and travel through the redwoods to **Willits** and back. Upon returning to Fort Bragg, head to the **Mendocino Coast Botanical Gardens** just down the road. It's the only public garden in the continental United States directly fronting the ocean. Mendocino is known for its fungi—the mushroom—and the gardens boast

some 80 varieties along with an abundance of flowers and plants.

Head back to the town of Mendocino to shop, visit art galleries, and take a peek inside the historic Mendocino Hotel. You can make your way down to the beach from near the Presbyterian Church on **Main Street** where stairs trail down to the shoreline.

Hop back in the car and drive south along Highway 1. You'll pass through Albion, a once thriving logging town, as you climb towards **Elk**. Pull off at the **Elk Cove Inn**

Organic Mendocino!

Mendocino County voted in 2003 to go GMO-free, banning all genetically modified organisms. Most everything you eat in the county is **organic, free-range and hormone free**.

and Spa for dinner. The inn's dining room has the most breathtaking views as well as a tantalizing menu.

ALTERNATIVE PLAN
The **North Coast** is the perfect setting to enjoy the great outdoors. Rent a canoe or kayak and take an adventure down the **Big River**, one of the only major undeveloped estuaries in Northern California. The route is made all the more interesting with its forested canyons, swimming holes and darting wildlife. You can rent equipment at various places, including Stanford Inn by the Sea.

THE CENTRAL COAST
It's one of California's most spectacular stretches of shoreline. Not only does it yield some of nature's most fascinating works—jutting promontories, pounding waves, and unusual rock formations awash with salt water—it also boasts some manmade scenery, including the hedonistic **Hearst Castle**.

From Mendocino to the Monterey Peninsula
Take Highway 128 back through the Anderson Valley to Highway 101. Heading south on Highway 101, you'll pass through Santa Rosa, past Sausalito, over the Golden Gate Bridge, and onward to the Monterey Peninsula exit where you'll merge onto Highway 156.

With only two days to spare, you need to decide what you want to accomplish along the Central Coast. If you want to visit **Hearst Castle**, then stay in Cambria and spend your two days exploring this behemoth. If you want to just hang out at the beach and spend your last couple of days doing nothing in particular, then hunker down in Santa Cruz. Unfortunately the Central Coast is just too expansive to experience in two days, so it's best you pick one area to explore.

Begin your visit with a trek along **17-Mile Drive**, which will take you along the magnificent coastline and through Pebble Beach. There are 21 optional stops, so pick those that appeal to you. Once you've completed your drive, head to the **Monterey Bay Aquarium**, located on Monterey's Cannery Row and touted as one of the nation's best aquariums. Explore the four largest exhibits: the Outer Bay, the Kelp Forest, Monterey Bay Habitats, and the Sea Otters along the Rocky Coast. Don't miss the walk-through aviary or the world's largest jelly fish galleries.

Next, head to the village of **Carmel** and stroll along **Ocean Avenue**. The street is lined with quaint shops tucked inside Hansel and Gretel-style buildings. At the

> **ALTERNATIVE PLAN**
> The aquarium could take a big chunk of your day and, let's face facts, you only have two days on the Monterey Peninsula. You could skip the aquarium and visit the **National Steinbeck Center** in nearby Salinas, which explores the life and works of writer John Steinbeck. The Central Coast was the inspiration for many of his stories, and his words have been brought to life through interactive exhibits, films and events. The nearby Steinbeck House, where the writer was born, is now a restaurant. *Info*: www.steinbeck.org. Tel. 831/796-3833. Salinas, One Main Street. Open daily 10am-5pm. Adults $10.95, children $7.95.

end of Ocean is the beach, a crescent-shaped shoreline that is better suited for admiring than sun bathing. Head back up Ocean Avenue towards town and jut off towards the residential areas where you'll find a mix of cottages, some modest

and some magnificent. Make your way to Lincoln and Seventh, just a block or two off Ocean Avenue, to the **Cypress Inn**. This charming property is owned by Doris Day, and it serves a wonderful **afternoon tea** in the lounge or courtyard.

If you do choose to spend your last day in San Jose, stay in the downtown area. I recommend the **San Jose Fairmont**, which is within walking distance to San Jose State University as well as many shops and restaurants in the downtown district. Nearby attractions include:
- Happy Hollow Park & Zoo
- The Winchester Mystery House
- Children's Discovery Museum
- Lick Observatory
- Santana Row shopping district
- San Jose Institute of Contemporary American Art
- Japanese American Museum

Don't Miss in Northern California ....

- **Coit Tower** in San Francisco
- **Wine tasting** along the Silverado Trail
- A **mud bath** in Calistoga
- **Kayaking** along the Big River in Mendocino
- A hair-raising ride aboard the **Giant Dipper** roller coaster in Santa Cruz
- A heady tour of **Hearst Castle**
- **Hiking** to Bridalveil Fall in **Yosemite** (Half Dome if you're more daring)
- A **sunset gondola ride** in Lake Tahoe to the viewing platform at **Heavenly Resort**
- Champagne tasting at **Korbel Champagne Cellars** in Guerneville
- **COPIA** in Napa

9. BEST SLEEPS & EATS

Northern California, especially San Francisco, has a high ratio of expensive hotels. You're likely to get a better nightly rate in the resort towns, such as Napa/Sonoma, on weekdays – especially during the off-season. Check the hotel websites to see what specials are offered.

Hotels are listed by city in alphabetical order. **Expensive listings receive three dollar signs** (rooms starting at $400 per night), **moderate hotels get two** (rates beginning at $175 nightly) and **budget properties earn just one** ($175 per night or less).

BEST SLEEPS

Clift $$$
The century-old Clift (*see photo on previous page*) received a new lease on life a few years back at the hands of Philippe Starck, the world renowned designer. The hotel is a mix of old-world elegance and contemporary glamour. The rooms are generously proportioned with floor-to-ceiling mirrors creating a roomier effect. *Info:* www.clifthotel.com. Tel. 800/652-5438. Union Square. 495 Geary St. 363 rooms/suites.

The Fairmont San Francisco $$$
Located atop exclusive Nob Hill at the crossroads of the Powell-Mason cable car line, The Fairmont is one of the city's most revered properties. With its distinct terra cotta façade and festoon of international flags, the hotel has hosted every president since William Howard Taft. A recent — and much needed — renovation has brought the property back to its original turn-of-the-century splendor. There are two wings, the original and a mid-century addition, where rooms and corridors definitely reek of old money. The hotel is also home to the elegant Laurel Court, where afternoon tea is enjoyed beneath a trio of ornate domes. The hotel's Tonga Room and Hurricane Bar are a bit kitsch, but unique none-the-less with impromptu thunder and tropical rainstorms. The hotel welcomes pets under 20 pounds. *Info:* www.fairmont.com. Tel. 800/441-1414. Nob Hill, 950 Mason St. 591 rooms/suites.

Hotel Monaco $$$
French-inspired architecture and an extremely playful décor is what makes a stay at Hotel Monaco a memorable experience. The hotel is eye-candy for anyone with an appreciation for design and aesthetics. The front desk resembles a steamer trunk, while the lobby features an ample-sized fireplace

and a whimsical frescoed ceiling. There is also a painting of the Celestial Lady that beckons from the grand staircase. There are 24 designer suites; "standard" rooms are equally interesting with their vibrant colors and abundant textures. Pets are welcome, too. *Info:* www.monaco-sf.com. Tel. 800/214-4220. Union Square, 501 Geary St. 201 rooms/suites.

The Huntington Hotel & Nob Hill Spa $$$

The elegant 1924 brick building that now houses The Huntington originally operated as a 12-story apartment building. Its setting

is formal and all rooms have views of the City, Huntington Park or Grace Cathedral coupled with wet bars or kitchens. A trip to the hotel's spa is certainly worth the money. Guests can also take advantage of the complimentary chauffeured sedan service, offered daily until 4pm, which provides transportation to various parts of the city. *Info:* www.huntingtonhotel.com. Tel. 415/474-5400. Nob Hill, 1075 California St. 135 rooms/suites.

Intercontinental Mark Hopkins San Francisco $$$

Opened in 1926, the Mark Hopkins is another one of the city's classic hotels. Situated at the crest of Nob Hill at the intersection of three cable car lines, you'll find a selection of classic rooms and suite offering magnificent city and bay views. Located on the 19th floor is the legendary **Top of the Mark**, where you can sip martinis near the heavens. *Info:* www.markhopkins.net. Tel. 415/392-3434. Nob Hill, 999 California St. 380 rooms/suites.

Palace Hotel $$$

The Palace Hotel, first opened in 1875, is a relic from San Francisco's old guard. While the hotel's public rooms are opulent, the recently renovated guest rooms are a bit more understated and inviting. A warm color scheme, mahogany furnishings, and 14-foot ceilings create a lofty feel. The hotel's fourth floor houses a health club with a sky-lit swimming pool, whirlpool, full-service spa, sauna and fitness center. *Info:* www.sfpalace.com. Tel. 415/ 512-1111- Union Square, Two New Montgomery St., 553 rooms/ suites.

San Francisco

The Prescott Hotel $$$
The Prescott Hotel is part of the stylish Kipton portfolio of properties. Until the company took possession, the hotel was a decent place to stay but nothing extraordinary. It has since gone from vintage to vanguard emerging as an elegant townhouse-style hotel in a great location. The hotel also has an on-site fitness center and is a pet-friendly property. *Info:* www.prescotthotel.com. Tel. 800/ 283-7322- Union Square, 545 Post St. 164 rooms/suites.

W San Francisco $$$
Located in the heart of the city's hip SoMa district, the hotel faces the beautiful Yerba Buena Gardens and is just a short jaunt from Union Square and the San Francisco Museum of Modern Art. The hotel, as with most W destinations, takes a minimalist approach when it comes to décor. Rooms are sleek, uncluttered and a bit cramped. Standard rooms are all located below the 12th floor, so if you want the same room with a better view you'll need to request a higher floor and expect to pay

Inn Above Tide

If you're limited on time but want to experience both San Francisco and the Wine Country, consider a stay at **Inn Above Tide** ($$$) in **Saulsalito**, just a quick ferry ride from the city and an hour car ride from the Wine Country. Once the fog lifts, the city's skyline quickly comes into view. Every room literally teeters above the water and most come with private balconies (request one – it's worth the few extra dollars). Other amenities include fireplaces and flat screen televisions, but all boast the most amazing views. *Info:* www.innabovetide.com. Tel. 800/893-8433. Sausalito (just on the other side of the Golden Gate Bridge and across the bay from San Francisco), 30 El Portal. 29 Rooms/Suites. Parking additional.

more for the privilege. There is also a heated lap pool on the premises. *Info:* www.whotels.com/sanfrancisco. Tel. 415/777-5300. Yerba Buena, 171 Third St. 410 rooms.

Argonaut Hotel $$

Located in the heart of Fisherman's Wharf, the Argonaut Hotel makes its home in the historic Haslett Warehouse at The Cannery. Behind the 1907 brick structure is a plush and stylish inn where you slumber just steps from the cable car turnaround, Ghiradelli Square, Pier 39 and other waterfront attractions. *Info:* www.argonauthotel.com, Tel. 415/563-0800. Fisherman's Wharf, 495 Jefferson St. at Hyde. 252 rooms/suites.

Hotel Drisco $$

Located in Pacific Heights is the 1903 Hotel Drisco, which is just a short jaunt via bus from Union Square, Fisherman's Wharf, the Financial District, and Fillmore Street's shops and eateries. From hardwood floors to ample-size poster beds, Hotel Drisco offers a relaxing place to nest in the heart of the urban swell. Complimentary breakfast buffet, evening wine, and coffee/tea service included. *Info:* www.hoteldrisco.com. Tel. 415/346-2880. Pacific Heights, 2901 Pacific Ave. 48 rooms/suites.

Inn at Union Square $$

The name says it all. Just a few steps off Union Square is this small and intimate inn. While the selection of rooms and suites are certainly adequate and pleasing, the hotel really does a superb job with its service. In the early evening there is wine and hors d'oeuvres served by a cozy fireplace. Other touches that make the inn a standout is evening turndown service, complimentary bottled water, free use of a nearby health center, overnight shoeshine service at no cost, and complimentary continental breakfast – all this for an extremely reasonable nightly rate. *Info:* www.unionsquare.com Tel. 800/288-4346. Union Square, 440 Post St. 30 rooms.

Kensington Park Hotel $$

I've been staying at this hotel for years, and I still consider it one of the best hotels for the value. The hotel combines a classic sense of style with some modern conveniences and is just steps from great shopping and dining. The rooms are spacious for a vintage hotel, and a recent renovation has resulted in a soothing color scheme and updated furnishings. Smokers must light up elsewhere as the Kensington Park Hotel is completely smoke-free. *Info:* www.kensingtonparkhotel.com. Tel. 800/553-1900. Union Square, 450 Post St. 89 rooms/suites.

San Francisco

Sir Francis Drake $$

If you never stay at the Sir Francis Drake, you'll come to know it by its trademark beefeater-clad doorman who stands outside the hotel's entrance on Powell Street. Built in 1928, the hotel is surprisingly elegant. The Mind. Body. Spa program allows for in-room spa services and complimentary yoga accessories to use during your stay. There is also the Forget It? We've Got It! plan where the hotel stocks the necessary travel essentials (toothpaste, tooth brushes, deodorant) that you may have left behind at home. Pets are also welcome. *Info:* www.sirfrancisdrake.com. Tel. 800/227-5480. Union Square, 450 Powell St. 417 rooms/suites.

Westin St. Francis $$

The St. Francis is a timeless hotel with an enviable location right on Union Square. Cable cars pass in front of the hotel day and night, and within walking distance are some of the best restaurants and shops in the city. The hotel is the marriage of two buildings,  the original 1904 structure and a more modern tower completed in the early 1970s. Depending on your preference, historic and charming or modern and functional, request your room accordingly. *Info:* www.westinstfrancis.com. Tel. 415/397-7000. Union Square, 335 Powell St. 1,195 rooms/suites.

Hotel California $

Until recently this was known as the Savoy Hotel. A name change and a few renovations later, this 92-year-old inn is looking good and is also a good bargain with charming rooms, 400-thread count linens and a convenient Theater District location. At check-in guests are welcomed with a free frozen tequila shot, and from 4-6pm every day is a wine and cheese reception. The Family Suite is actually a great bargain at about $220 a night. *Info:* www.hotelca.com. Tel. 800/227-4223- Union Square, 580 Geary St. 82 rooms/suites.

Hotel Diva $

This sleek, modern retreat is simple and sexy with a striking color scheme and great address. Rooms are ultra-modern with eye-popping cobalt blue carpeting set against varied tones of gray, black and stainless steel appointments. The hotel also offers its "Little Divas Suite," an adjoining room for kids decked out in vibrant colors of red, flamingo pink and bursts of yellow outfitted with colorful futons, oversized cushions and a drawing table. The room is also equipped with a karaoke machine, a trunk filled with dress-up clothes, and a CD player. *Info:* www.hoteldiva.com. Tel. 800/552-1900. Union Square, 440 Geary St. 111 rooms/suites.

Hotel Triton $

While the names of celebrity guests trill off the tongues of hotel managers elsewhere, Hotel Triton has created a handful of suites either inspired or actually created by the celebrity themselves. My favorite? Kathy Griffin's D-List Suite, designed by the comedienne and Mike Nielsen, someone she refers to as her "gay visionary." Not to be missed is the evening wine party (especially Friday nights when a DJ is on hand) with tarot card readings and chair massages. *Info:* www.hoteltriton.com. Tel. 800/433-6611. Union Square/Chinatown, 342 Grant Ave. 140 rooms/suites.

Hotel Union Square $

The lobby of this 1913 hotel was recently renovated in the Art Deco style and it recently unveiled the Dashiell Hammett Suite, a room dedicated to frequent guest and author of the 1930 novel *The Maltese Falcon.* The hotel's location is its best asset: Walk out the main entrance and you're right in the heart of Union Square and just a block from the cable car turnaround. *Info:* www.hotelunionsquare.com. Tel. 800/553-1900. Union Square, 114 Powell St. 131 rooms/suites.

Maxwell Hotel $

Built in 1908, the Maxwell is a smart boutique property located near
the Theater District. The Art Deco influences create a bold statement in what could otherwise be a non-descript hotel. The rooms
are small, but stylish. Complimentary morning coffee and tea is
available in the lobby, and guests enjoy room service from Max's on
the Square – a New York-style deli. There is also free Wi-Fi and
complimentary newspapers. *Info:* www.maxwellhotel.com. Tel.
415/986-2000. Union Square, 386 Geary St. 153 rooms/suites.

San
Francisco

Hotel Vertigo $

This hotel gained some fame a few decades back as the setting for
Alfred Hitchcock's thriller "Vertigo." Now that the cobwebs
have been dusted off and the dizziness has subsided, the former
York Hotel has emerged a chic Edwardian-style inn with newly
remodeled rooms and suites boasting flat screen televisions and
wireless Internet connection. Daily continental breakfast is served
in the lobby, and pets are also welcome. The hotel, which at press
time was slated for a name change to Hotel Vertigo, is also home
to the Empire Plush Room, a former speakeasy that is now one of
the city's most celebrated cabarets. *Info:* www.yorkhotel.com.
Tel. 800/808-9675. Nob Hill, 940 Sutter St. 96 rooms/suites.

BEST EATS
Asia de Cuba $$$

Located behind the doors of
the Clift hotel is this celebrated
restaurant known for its innovative global cuisine and glamorous digs festooned with silk
curtains, mahogany and leather
banquettes, hand-blown
Murano glass lamps, and a
symbolic cross-shaped communal table that is both mir-
rored and illuminated. *Info*:
www.morganshotelgroup.com. Tel. 415/929-2300. Union Square,
495 Geary Street.

Big 4 Restaurant $$$

Located inside the Huntington Hotel and named for the big four railroad tycoons—Stanford, Hopkins, Crocker, Huntington— this clubby, old-school restaurant offers a very innovative menu. The nightly Wild Game Dish has featured everything from ostrich to alligator. A great stop for a pre or post-meal cocktail. *Info:* www.big4restaurant.com. Tel. 415/771-1140. Nob Hill, 1075 California St.

The Garden Court $$$

Dine beneath a breathtaking dome of stained glass at one of the city's most admired dining rooms with its dangling chandeliers and sleek marble columns. The breakfast and lunch menus feature classic California cuisine, but it's the ritual of Saturday afternoon tea that really makes an elegant statement. *Info:* www.gardencourt-restaurant.com. Tel. 415/512-1111. Union Square, Palace Hotel - Two New Montgomery St.

One Market Restaurant $$$

Catering to San Francisco's well-heeled business crowd, One Market Restaurant is open for both lunch and dinner in the heart of the Financial District. The restaurant boasts an exhibition kitchen with a "chef's table" located behind the kitchen door, a sleek bar, and a fabulous menu of contemporary and seasonal American dishes. Seafood is purchased in the morning from local fisherman, while area ranchers provide the fresh beef and poultry. *Info:* www.onemarket.com. Tel. 415/777-5577. Embarcadero, 1 Market St.

Eat at the Ferry Building

If you're looking for one-stop dining, head to the fabulous **Ferry Building Marketplace** at the Embarcadero. Likened to an American version of a London food hall, you'll find nearly every cuisine represented in a casual yet culinary atmosphere. There are bread and cheese shops, cafes and small eateries, a trio of restaurants, wine bars, and ice cream and gelato stalls. This truly is one of my favorite city stops.

The Slanted Door
$$$

San Francisco

This modern Vietnamese restaurant is a local favorite that weds traditional flavors with local ingredients. Located in the famed Ferry Building Marketplace, the menu is a celebration of culture with a Riesling-driven wine list and a full bar. Lunch, dinner and an afternoon Asian tea are served daily. *Info:*www.slanteddoor.com. Tel. 415/861-8032. Embarcadero, One Ferry Building.

Asia SF $$

This is certainly one of the city's more lively restaurants and the only one I know of where gender illusionists perform hourly and also moonlight as servers. The Cal-Asian menu of satay and seafood is stellar, but the over-the-top ambiance is even more appetizing at this never-ending party. *Info:*www.asiasf.com. Tel. 415/ 434-4204. South of Market, 201 Ninth St.

Bistro Boudin Restaurant and Bar $$

With great views of the bay and Alcatraz Island, Boudin's is a nice place to dine along the waterfront. The restaurant serves up a medley of classic cuisine including fresh fish, clam chowder served in Boudin's trademark sourdough bowl, and chicken and beef dishes along with sandwiches, salads and more. A full bar and children's menu are available plus free admission to the bakery and museum tour is included with your meal. If you want to grab just a sandwich, salad or soup, the first floor café offers counter service and limited indoor/outdoor seating. *Info:* www.boudinbakery.com. Tel. 415/928-1849. Fisherman's Wharf, 160 Jefferson.

Calzones $$

Located in North Beach, this European-style bistro offers just a scattering of tables and booths insides its pizza-slice shaped dining room. You can also opt to sit along the sidewalk to graze on such specialties as a crab melt sandwich along with a selection of salads, risotto, pasta, and rustic pizzas. *Info:* www.calzonesf.com. Tel. 415/397-3600. North Beach, 430 Columbus Ave.

Citizen Cake $$

This full-service eatery, bar and patisserie serves up a fabulous

array of items for breakfast, lunch and dinner. Pressed sandwiches, mouthwatering salads and an array of seafood and chops offer something for everyone. Desserts are especially decadent. *Info:*www.citizencake.com. Tel. 415/861-2228. Hayes Valley, 399 Grove St.

First Crush Restaurant, Wine Bar and Lounge $$

This dinner-only, white tablecloth bistro features an amazing menu of French-American fare coupled with more than 400 California wines. Select from a creative menu of appetizers, salads and entrees, or have nothing more than a glass of wine and a cheese plate. *Info:* www.firstcrush.com. Tel. 415/982-7874. Union Square, 101 Cyril Magnin.

Shanghai 1930 $$

Taking its cue from when Shanghai was known as the "Paris of the Orient," this very stylish restaurant features live jazz, a fabulous selection of dim sum, Cantonese specialties and other Asian dishes. Lovely atmosphere for both lunch and dinner. *Info:* www.shanghai1930.com. Tel. 415/896-5600. Embarcadero, 133 Steuart St.

Steps of Rome Trattoria $$

With a nod to the trattorias of Rome, this charming North Beach dinner-only eatery features a selection of antipasti, salads, veal, grilled lamb and pasta dishes paired with a stellar wine list. For a more casual experience, the café next door serves up less formal fare, such as paninis, pasta, pizza and some of the strongest espresso in town. *Info:*www.stepsofrome.com. Tel. 415/986-6480. North Beach, 362 Columbus Ave.

Tokyo Go Go $$

Located in the Mission District, you'll nosh among local sushi devotees. Check out the weekday Handroll Happy Hour, as well as the sake sampler, which seem to be among the most ordered items. *Info:* www.toykogogo.com. Tel. 415/864-2288. Mission District, 3174 16th St.

San Francisco

Café de la Presse $

This charming French-inspired bistro is located in the shadow of Chinatown's ornate dragon gates. With a nod to Parisian culture, guests are encouraged to enjoy the age-old pastime of dining and conversing about everyday life. Open for breakfast, lunch and dinner, this casual and informal café features everything from pâté and flakey quiche to grilled sandwiches. *Info:* www.cafedelapresse.com. Tel. 415/398-2680. Union Square, 352 Grant Ave.

Cliff House Bistro $

Situated in a 1909 structure that seems suspended above the bay, the Cliff House is a symbol of historic San Francisco. Breathtaking

views of the Pacific Ocean and Marin County coastline come into view once the fog lifts. The restaurant offers casual dining for breakfast, lunch and dinner with mouthwatering omelets, sandwiches, and fresh seafood. *Info:* www.cliffhouse.com. Tel. 415/386-3330. Ocean Beach/Zoo, 1090 Point Lobos Ave.

Emporior Rulli Gran Caffe $

This stylish café, pastry shop and wine bar is a neighborhood favorite and offers affordable food and inviting ambiance. The selection of homemade pasta, pizza and sandwiches, coupled with cheese and meat plates, are simple and satisfying. Breakfast, which includes a morning pizza, is also available as well as generous servings of cappuccino. *Info:* www.rulli.com. Tel. 415/ 923-6464. The Marina, 2300 Chestnut St.

Max's Opera Café $
This New York-style deli, located near the opera house, serves up generous portions of both Puccini and pastrami. That's because the wait staff takes turns performing on the small stage between food runs. The menu embodies classic deli fare, from bagels and lox to thick Rueben sandwiches on rye. *Info:* www.maxsworld.com. Tel. 415/771-7300. Van Ness, 601 Van Ness Ave.

Nordstrom Bistro $
You can work up quite an appetite prowling for a pair of Jimmy Choo's, so when hunger strikes head to the top floor of Nordstrom. This fashionable café offers breathtaking views, freshly made sandwiches, salads, and pastas, as well as some rather calorie-laden deserts which, by the way, can easily be worked off as you traipse from boutique to boutique. *Info:* www.nordstrom.com. Tel. 415/977-5155. Union Square, 865 Market St.

Sears Fine Food $
With long lines trailing down Powell Street, Sears is a San Francisco breakfast destination. Serving airy pancakes and traditional egg dishes, along with sandwiches, salads and steaks for lunch and dinner, Sears offers a convenient location and reasonably-priced menu. *Info:* www.searsfinefood.com. Tel. 415/986-1160. Union Square, 439 Powell St.

Utopia Café $
Known for its authentic Hong Kong clay pot dishes, salt and pepper fish, and wonton soup, Utopia Café is located in the heart of Chinatown. A favorite of locals, you'll find the food reasonably priced and the setting authentic. *Info:* www.utopiacafesf.com. Tel. 415/956-2902- Chinatown, 139 Waverly Pl.

HALF MOON BAY

BEST SLEEPS
The Ritz-Carlton $$$
This is the area's only full-service resort and it lives up to its ritzy

reputation. Although new in design, the resort evokes a bygone era with its postcard perfect views of the California coastline, luxe accommodations, stellar dining options, spa services, and 36-hole championship golf course. Be prepared to pay nearly $40 a night for valet parking. *Info:* www.ritzcarlton.com. Tel. 650/ 712-7000. Half Moon Bay, One Miramontes Point Rd. 261 rooms/ suites.

Half Moon Bay

Wine Country

Seal Cove Inn $$
Part of the Four Sisters Inn portfolio of charming properties, the Seal Cove Inn borders the park and ocean in nearby Moss Beach making it convenient for outdoor adventure. Guests rooms are nicely sized with king beds, fireplaces, and private baths coupled with either terraces or balconies boasting distant ocean views. Your stay includes a full breakfast, afternoon tea and hors d'oeuvres, and home-baked cookies before bedtime. *Info:* www.sealcoveinn.com. Tel. 800/995-9987. Moss Beach, 221 Cypress Av. 10 rooms.

BEST EATS
Cetrella Bistro & Cafe $$
A stylish restaurant with private dining and live jazz featuring fresh seafood and pasta, plus a stellar cheese and dessert menu with recommended wine pairings. *Info:* www.cetrella.com. Tel. 650/726-4090. Half Moon Bay, 845 Main St.

Moonside Bakery & Café $
This European-style bakery is an ideal place for breakfast or lunch with its selection of artisan breads, wood-fired pizzas, hearty sandwiches and creative salads. Those with a sweet tooth will also enjoy the full-line of bakery items, from cookies and tarts to delicious slices of cake and pie. *Info:* www.moonsidebakery.com. Tel. 650/726-9070. Half Moon Bay, 604 Main St.

WINE COUNTRY: NAPA & SONOMA

BEST SLEEPS
The Carneros Inn $$$
San Francisco mayor Gavin Newsom is one of the partners of this

resort and, like the man himself, this Napa Valley hideaway causes quite a stir. The collection of casually elegant cottages, averaging 1000 square feet, offers optimal seclusion that combines comfort with convenience. Behind closed doors you'll find wood-burning fireplaces, flat-panel televisions, and floors covered in Brazilian cherry wood. You'll also have shower options — indoor or al fresco — it's up to you. The resort, nestled among the vineyards, features a fabulous restaurant, elongated swimming pool, spa and secluded location. *Info:* www.thecarnerosinn.com. Tel. 707/299-4900. Napa, 4048 Sonoma Highway. 86 cottages/suites.

The Fairmont Sonoma Mission Inn & Spa $$$

With its trademark salmon-colored façade and signature tower hovering at cloud level, the historic Fairmont Sonoma Mission Inn & Spa is an idyllic retreat with elegantly-appointed rooms, fine dining, a gracious golf course, spa, swimming pool and every other full-service convenience imaginable. Teetering on the edge of Sonoma proper, the resort is an ideal getaway for both romantics and those traveling with kids. Guests can partake in the daily afternoon wine tasting. *Info:* www.fairmont.com/sonoma. Tel. 707/939-2400. Boyes Hot Springs, 100 Boyes Blvd. 226 rooms/suites.

Kenwood Inn & Spa $$$

Looking as if it were plucked from the Tuscan countryside is this fabulous inn offering the ultimate romantic wine country get-

away. Celebrity guests are known to sequester themselves behind the doors of this cloistered inn where more than two-dozen rooms and suites with sweeping vineyard views are located in a trio of separate courtyards. Each abode is uniquely appointed with ambient lighting, original artwork, and plush furnishings. The inn is also home to a restaurant and wine bar, two swimming pools, and a world-class spa. *Info:* www.kenwoodinn.com. Tel. 707/833-1293. Kenwood, 10400 Sonoma Highway. 30 rooms/suites.

MacArthur Place $$$

Situated on a former winery just a few blocks from the historic Sonoma Plaza is this elegant vintage-style inn. The collection of rooms is housed in mostly two-story, white clapboard buildings boasting such features as luxe furnishings, ample-size bathrooms, fireplaces, patios and porches. Flagstone walkways meander past fountains and flora to the swimming pool, spa and restaurant. A complimentary buffet breakfast is served each morning inside Spurs, the hotel's restaurant, and complimentary wine is poured each evening in the library and courtyard. *Info:* www.macarthurplace.com. Tel. 707/938-2929. Sonoma, 29 East MacArthur St. 64 rooms/suites.

Wine Country

Meadowood Resort $$$

Located on a winding road just off the famed Silverado Trail is this wondrous, country club-style retreat. Scattered throughout the many acres are cozy cottages clinging to hillsides and shaded by the branches of mature trees. The resort features both an adults-only and family pool, spa, fine dining, croquet, tennis and golf. Each evening guests are invited to join the resort's wine experts for a tasting of two outstanding Napa Valley wines. The resort's wine experts will also help you plot out your wine trail adventure, pointing out some of the better vintners to visit. *Info:* www.meadowood.com. Tel. 800/458-8080. St. Helena, 900 Meadowood Ln. 85 cottages/suites/lodges.

1801 First $$

Located near Napa's historic downtown district is this luxurious bed and breakfast inn featuring a handful of suites in the main house plus a pair of adjoining cottages and additional quarters in the Carriage House. The landmark Queen Anne Victorian home was built in 1903 and is a departure from the traditional bed and breakfast with its blend of classic architecture and sophisticated décor. All rooms have romantic fireplaces, sitting areas, televisions and CD players. The rate includes breakfast, evening wine and hors d'oeuvres plus complimentary 24/7 mini bar access. *Info:* www.1801first.com. Tel. 707/224-3739. Downtown Napa, 1801 First St. 8 suites/cottages.

Cottage Grove Inn $$$

What was once a former trailer park has been cleared of all doublewides and is now home to a row of neatly-lined, stylish cottages. Relax on your own front porch rocking away in a cozy chair while enjoying complimentary wine and cheese. Each two-person cottage features a wood-burning fireplace, deep soaking tub and stylish surroundings. You can also walk to downtown Calistoga restaurants, spas and galleries. *Info:* www.cottagegroveinn.com. Tel. 707/942-8400. Calistoga, 1711 Lincoln Ave. 16 cottages.

Healdsburg Inn on the Plaza $$

Built in 1901 and overlooking the town plaza, this former turn-of-the-century bank offers an inviting ambiance and on-the-square location. Each chamber is individually appointed with some rooms opening up onto private or common terraces. Expect high ceilings, original moldings, fireplaces, exposed brick walls, and warm hospitality provided by the staff. Breakfast and evening wine are included and served in the second-floor dining room. *Info:* www.healdsburginn.com. Tel. 800/431-8663- Healdsburg, 112 Matheson St. 12 rooms/suites.

Le Petites Maisons $$

Located behind the gourmet Fig Pantry are a cluster of four, cozy cottages situated a mile from the historic Sonoma Plaza. These homes away from home include separate kitchens, living areas and bedrooms. The quartet shares a common garden complete with a bubbling fountain and picnic tables with umbrellas. Cottages are available nightly or weekly, and daily housekeeping is an additional charge. Barbecues and bikes are included in the nightly rate. *Info:* www.thegirlandthefig.com. Tel. 707/933-0340. Sonoma, 1190 East Napa St. 4 cottages.

The Lodge at Sonoma $$

This Renaissance Resort and Spa offers a perfect escape for the entire family. The inn is located at a busy intersection, but once inside you feel completely shielded from the outside world. There are an abundance of cottages, suites and lodge accommodations boasting such features as fireplaces and French doors leading to private patios and balconies. On the premises are a wine tasting room, restaurant, spa and swimming pool. It's a bit of a hike to the historic plaza, but it's doable. *Info:* www.thelodgeatsonoma.com. Tel. 707/935-6600. Sonoma, 1325 Broadway. 186 rooms/suites/cottages.

Wine Country

Napa Valley Railway Inn $
Sitting on original track that was once the Napa Valley Railroad, this unique inn allows you to travel back in time to the opulent era of railroad barons. You'll actually slumber inside a vintage railcar or caboose suite, which are small and simply decorated with king or queen beds plus sitting areas and private baths. Rooms also include flat screen televisions and small refrigerators. There is no lobby or common areas, but the town of Yountville is just beyond your sleeper car door. *Info:* www.napavalleyrailwayinn.com. Tel. 707/944-2000. Yountville, 6503 Washington St. 9 vintage railcars.

BEST EATS
Dry Creek Kitchen $$$
Celebrity chef Charlie Palmer serves some 600 Sonoma County-only wines at his stylish eatery located on Healdsburg scenic town plaza. With a focus on simple food and ingredients plucked from the farms of Sonoma County, the ever-changing menu of wine country cuisine makes securing a reservation difficult at times. Be patient, it's well worth it. *Info:* www.charliepalmer.com. Tel. 707/431-0330. Healdsburg, 317 Healdsburg Ave.

The French Laundry $$$
Perhaps one of the nation's most acclaimed restaurants — and one of the hardest to score a last-minute reservation — Chef Thomas Keller has created a fabulous find in the heart of Napa. This former French laundry, hence the name, was built in 1900 and offers an intimate dining experience for dinner or weekend lunch. There are two menus available that change on a daily basis: the nine-course Chef's Tasting Menu and the nine-course Vegetable

Menu Tasting priced at $240 per person inclusive of service charge. Reservations are taken two months in advanced. *Info:* www.frenchlaundry.com. Tel. 707/944-2380. Yountville, 6640 Washington St.

Julia's Kitchen $$

Named for one of the culinary arts most iconic figures, Julia Child, and located at COPIA, the American Center for Wine, Food and the Arts, this wondrous eatery offers a perfect blend of fine food and a relaxed setting. The flavorful California-French fare uses ingredients pulled from the center's own organic garden. From fresh seafood and foie gras to a splendid cheese course, Ms. Child would feel right at home. *Info:* www.juliaskitchen.com. Tel. 707/265-5700. Napa, 500 First St.

Bouchon

Can't score a reservation at the coveted French Laundry? Well, don't despair. You can dine next-door at Chef Keller's other highly-acclaimed restaurant **Bouchon**. Housed in an historic 1800s Wells Fargo stagecoach stop, this French bistro's menu won't take you to the cleaners. *Info:* www.bouchonbistro.com. Tel. 707/944-8037. Yountville, 6534 Washington St.

Market $$

Located in an historic building with the top of the back bar pulled from The Palace Hotel in San Francisco at the height of prohibition, this stylish American bistro, with its soaring ceilings and exposed brick walls, features lunch and dinner menus that highlight seasonal ingredients from the area's many local purveyors. The menu changes often, but rarely, if ever, disappoints. *Info:* www.marketsthelena.com. Tel. 707/963-3799. St. Helena, 1347 Main St.

Santi $$

This local treasure is an ode to the Italian settlers that founded the region. The menu is a celebration of old-world specialties with just the mildest hint of nouveau. The dining room is lively and, unlike some of Sonoma and Napa's other eateries, the service is decent but nothing over-the-top. The wine list is impressive and offers both local vintages as well as those from "the boot." *Info:* www.tavernasanti.com. Tel. 707/ 857-1790. Geyersville, 21047 Geyersville Ave.

The Girl and The Fig $$

A Sonoma staple, this inviting bistro features a welcoming antique bar where French aperitifs and thirst-quenching spirits are served. The seasonal menu, cheese and charcuterie platters, along with the selection of fresh fish, creative sandwiches and starter items are always palate-pleasing. The outdoor patio offers the best seats in the house. *Info:* www.thegirlandthefig.com. Tel. 707/938-3634. Sonoma, 110 West Spain St.

Oakville Grocery $

With its umbrella-laden patio and a feast of favorites found inside the store's deli, this wine country favorite offers one-stop shopping for picky picnickers and stay-put diners. There's a long list of gourmet pastas, handmade cheeses, market-fresh sandwiches and salads. Check-out the weekly paella night, which gets cooking every Thursday. *Info:* www.oakvillegrocery.com. Tel. 707/433-3200. Healdsburg, 124 Matheson.

THE CENTRAL COAST

BEST SLEEPS
Casa Palermo $$$

With just two dozen spacious rooms and suites, this romantic Mediterranean-style enclave is situated on the first and second fairways of the famed Pebble Beach Golf Links. Curl up beside the wood-burning fireplace behind your guest room door or read the newspaper on your private patio overlooking the course. Complimentary evening refreshments served in the intimate bar. *Info:* www.pebblebeach.com. Tel. 831/622-6650. Pebble Beach, 1518 Cypress Dr. 24 rooms/suites.

The Old Monterey Inn $$$

This historic bed and breakfast foregoes the chintz and teddy bears opting for a more sophisticated approach to hospitality.

The inviting rooms and suites, coupled with incredible gardens and a spa sanctuary, make this an ideal choice for those in search of something more than just a place to sleep. The rate includes a full gourmet breakfast, afternoon refreshments and evening hors d'oeuvres served with complimentary wine and beverages. *Info:* www.oldmontereyinn.com. Tel. 831/375-8284. Monterey, 500 Martin St. 10 rooms/suites.

The Orchid Inn at San Simeon $$
Located near Hearst Castle and just five minutes from the village of Cambria, this stylish inn offers attractive accommodations in an economical wing and a pricier, more luxurious wing. There is a pool on the premises, though the area tends to be a bit chilly most months, as well as a restaurant, lounge and spa. Pets are welcome, too. *Info:* www.orchidinnatsansimeon.com. Tel. 800/451-9900. San Simeon. 55 rooms/suites.

Tradewinds Carmel $$$
Offering a departure from Carmel's Hansel & Gretel architecture is this Zen-like sanctuary. Its Asian influences offers tranquility among its collection of plush and minimalist chambers. You'll find poetically chic rooms with a fusion of Asian, Balinese and tropical designs with Kimono robes to lounge in. A continental breakfast buffet is included, or you can stroll a short distance down to the village for an early morning cup of coffee. *Info:* www.tradewindscarmel.com. Tel. 831/624-2776. Carmel, Mission St. at Third. 28 rooms/suites.

Chaminade $$
Situated on a scenic mountain ridge, this stunning retreat offers commanding views of the bay and hills. Just five minutes from the Santa Cruz Boardwalk, beaches and downtown, this average-sized resort features contemporary Spanish décor behind chamber doors with a touch of whimsy at times. You'll find tennis

courts, a swimming pool, spa services and two restaurants on the premises. *Info:* www.chaminade.com. Tel. 800/283-6569. Santa Cruz, One Chaminade Ln. 156 rooms/suites.

Cypress Inn $$
This Mediterranean hideaway, with its garden courtyard and inviting lobby bar, is owned by actress and pet activist Doris Day. Located amid the village area near all the shops, galleries and restaurants, a stay here is a guaranteed enjoyment. The rooms vary in size, shape and location with some having courtyard and snippet ocean views while other are warmed by fireplaces. A new hotel wing houses the plushest of the lot. Pets, of course, are welcome to stay with their owners. *Info:* www.cypress-inn.com. Tel. 831/624-3871- Carmel, Lincoln and Seventh. 44 rooms/suites.

Consider Big Sur

Central Coast

If your only interest in visiting the Central Coast is for its beauty, then consider staying in **Big Sur**, a 40 minute drive from Carmel along the sometimes treacherous Highway 1. Defined by jagged cliffs and a rugged coastline several feet below, this is one of the state's most beautiful and unspoiled stretches. There are several places to stay, including the very exclusive **Post Ranch Inn** and **Ventana Inn and Spa**, to more affordable spots like **Deetjen's Big Sur Inn** where you can opt to share a bath or request a cottage with private facilities. There are also an abundance of campgrounds if you prefer to go that route. *Info:* www.bigsurcalifornia.org.

Highlands Inn, Park Hyatt Carmel $$
It was reported that Sean Penn and Madonna honeymooned here after their 1985 wedding. Teetering above Point Lobos, about four miles south of Carmel, this rustically elegant find houses clusters of guest rooms in terraced buildings where decks and balconies make the most of the fabulous views. The resort also features a pair of restaurants, a swimming pool, and a secluded location. *Info:* www.highlandsinn.hyatt.com. Tel. 831/620-1234. Carmel, 120 Highlands Dr. 142 rooms/suites.

Central
Coast

La Playa Hotel $$
Situated a few blocks from the village of Carmel sits this historic and unassuming property. This former century-old Mediterranean villa boasts cozy rooms that are small but romantic with snapshot ocean views, an intimate lobby retreat, blooming gardens, fine dining and a swimming pool. The cluster of cottages is located about a block away and yields added privacy. *Info:* www.laplayahotel.com. Tel. 831/624-6476. Carmel, Camino Real at Eighth. 75 room/suites, 5 cottages.

Quail Lodge Resort & Golf Club $$
Nestled on 850 acres in the valley area of Carmel, Quail Lodge is an intimate retreat with less than 100 rooms. The grounds are

punctuated with placid lakes and greenery making it all the more enchanting. Rooms are extremely comfortable and plush, but with no formal trappings often found at other such resorts. Kick back on the balcony or unwind in an oversized tub. Play golf, hit the spa, take a dip in the pool or enjoy dinner at the resort restaurant. *Info:* www.quaillodge.com. Tel. 888.828-8787. Carmel Valley, 8205 Valley Greens Dr. 97 rooms/suites.

West Cliff Inn $$
This new bed and breakfast inn, housed in a stately Italianate Victorian home rising three stories, sits on an imposing bluff across from the beach. The nine guest rooms all boast different features, from fireplaces to jetted spa tubs. Full breakfast served each morning plus wine and snacks in the afternoon. *Info:* www.westcliffinn.com. Tel. 800/979-0910. Santa Cruz, 174 West Cliff Dr. 9 rooms/suites.

Babbling Brook Inn $
Located a short drive from the chaos of the Santa Cruz boardwalk is this terraced bed and breakfast inn punctuated with cascading

waterfalls and shaded by mature pine and redwood trees. The rooms are named for famed artists and offer an array of comforts including fireplaces and spa tubs. Morning and evening food and beverage service is included. *Info:* www.innsbythesea.com. Tel. 831/427-2437. Santa Cruz, 1025 Laurel St. 13 rooms/suites.

Cambria Pines Lodge $
This simple, no frills inn located on a knoll overlooking Cambria's East Village area offers extensive gardens, motel-style rooms and an annex of newer luxury chambers and suites that are a couple of years old. There are also freestanding cottages, which make for a cozy stay. They have a restaurant and there is usually live jazz in the lounge. *Info:* www.cambriapineslodge.com. Tel. 805/927-4200. Cambria, 2905 Burton Dr. 153 rooms/suites/cabins.

Green Gables Inn $
This Queen Anne Victorian estate, built in 1888, offers spectacular views of the bay from most of its private and public rooms. Each chamber is individually decorated, from lustrous mahogany walls to plump canopy beds to a ladder that accesses the cozy attic bedroom. The inn's

San Jose's Best!

Central Coast

The Fairmont San Jose is located in the heart of San Jose's business and entertainment district and is a fabulous property if you have any interest in seeing the sights of the city, such as the Winchester Mystery House. From here it's also just a short drive to Santa Cruz and its attractions. Not to be missed is the elegant Sunday Brunch in the hotel's Fountain Restaurant. *Info*: www.fairmont.com/sanjose, Tel. 408/998-1900.

Cordevalle, located in the hidden hamlet of San Martin near Gilroy, the self-proclaimed garlic capitol, is a luxurious retreat with its own golf course, winery and award-winning restaurant. Service is superb and the selection of bungalows and villas is over the top. The welcome amenity alone — a complimentary bottle of the resort's Clos LaChance 2003 Cordevalle Cuvee and fresh fruit — is a fabulous way to begin or end your Northern California sojourn. *Info*: www.cordevalle.com, Tel. 408/695-4500.

Central Coast

Carriage House offers the most spacious of accommodations with a sitting area, king bed, fireplace and jetted spa tub. Breakfast and nightly snacks included in the rate. *Info:* www.greengablesinnpg. Tel. 800/722-1774. Pacific Grove, 301 Ocean View Blvd. 11 rooms.

Inn at Depot Hill $

This former Southern Pacific Railroad Depot, built in 1901, has been transformed and expanded into one of the area's finest bed and breakfast inns. Located one town over from Santa Cruz, the inn's dozen rooms recalls European train travel through such themed chambers as St. Tropez, Paris, and Portofino. Morning and evening food and beverage service is available on the patio or in the privacy of your room. *Info:* www.innsbythesea.com. Tel. 831/462-3376. Capitola, 250 Monterey Ave. 12 rooms/suites.

BEST EATS

Bouchée Restaurant & Wine Bar $$$

This stylish, dinner-only bistro offers select classic dishes using regional influences of the Monterey Coast. Steamed mussels served with pommes frites, foie gras, and black truffle tortellini are just a few of the entrees you'll find on the menu. The wine list is extensive with many vintages offered by the glass. *Info:* www.boucheecarmel.com. Tel. 831/626-7880. Carmel, Mission St. between Ocean & Seventh.

Sierra Mar $$$

It's difficult to decide what is more appetizing, the food or the views. The restaurant, located at the Post Ranch Inn, features

an innovative, four-course, prix fixe menu that changes daily depending on what's in season. Open for both lunch and dinner, you'll usually find fresh fish, a savory soup or salad, and pasta, beef or game. The fourth course is a fabulous dessert, and the wine list ain't too shabby either.

Info: www.postranchinn.com. Tel. 831/667-2200. Big Sur, Highway 1.

Shadowbrook Restaurant $$$
The best and most fun way to reach this creekside restaurant is via the hillside cable car tram that ferries diners up and down the steep slope. Located right on the Soquel Creek, the restaurant is charming with its legion of indoor/outdoor dining rooms. The menu features seafood, pasta and steak coupled with a selection of nightly specials. Kids menu available. *Info:* www.shadowbrookcapitola.com. Tel. 831/475-1511- Capitola, 1750 Wharf Rd.

The Tap Room $$$
Located at The Lodge at Pebble Beach is this clubby restaurant offering hearty fare, such as roasted prime rib and thick, juicy burgers. An outstanding selection of both draft and bottled beer is available. The setting is really lovely, and much less expensive than the other restaurants located within this Pebble Beach compound. *Info:* www.pebblebeach.com. Tel. 831/625-8525. Pebble Beach, 1700 17-Mile Dr.

La Bicyclette Restaurant $$
This rustic café, where the menu is handwritten on a chalkboard that hangs from the wall, is a wonderful dining destination. Open for lunch and dinner, as well as for late afternoon wine tasting, coffee and dessert, La Bicyclette is an inviting French bistro with a focus on local, fresh and organic ingredients. *Info:* www.labicycletterestaurant.com. Tel. 831/622-9899. Carmel, Dolores St. at Seventh.

The Brambles Dinner House $$
This local Cambria favorite has been serving dinner for more than a half century behind the doors of an historic clapboard home. The Bramble's menu puts a focus on fresh seafood, poultry, pasta, vegetarian and an assortment of Greek dishes. The wine list has a long listing of local vintages. *Info:* www.bramblesdinnerhouse.com. Tel. 805/927-4716. Cambria, 4005 Burton Dr.

Clouds Downtown $$
This upscale, unpretentious dining destination located in down-

town Santa Cruz offers creative American fare amid an artsy ambiance. Nibble on prime tenderloin of beef wrapped with proscuitto or check out the local catch served with soba noodles. Open for lunch and dinner. *Info:* www.cloudsdowntown.com. Tel. 831/429-2000. Santa Cruz, 110 Church St.

The Fishwife $$

This casual and reasonably-priced restaurant located in Pacific Grove offers the freshest fish, as well as some dishes for those who prefer that their food doesn't swim. The restaurant is a local relic dating back to the 1830s when a sailor's wife ran a small market known for its New England clam chowder. Kids are welcome, and the menu features the same items as their adult counterparts only served in appropriate-sized portions. *Info:* www.fishwife.com. Tel. 831/375-7107. Pacific Grove, 1996 1/2 Sunset Dr.

The Sow's Ear $$

This wood-paneled place, sandwiched among the shops and eateries of Cambria's charming village, serves contemporary California cuisine, such as fried brie and baguette, a tempting Chinese chicken salad, and the comforts of chicken fried steak. Ask for a seat by the fireplace, as well as a recommendation from the decent wine list. *Info:* www.thesowsear.com. Tel. 805/927-4865. Cambria, 2248 Main St.

The Crown & Anchor $

Located below street level and seemingly ripped from the streets of London is this authentic and enjoyable British pub in downtown Monterey. All the usual suspects are found on the menu, from fish and chips to cottage pie. You'll also find some more mainstream offerings, like New York steak and a flavorful Cobb salad. And, of course, the selection of beer won't disappoint. *Info:* www.crownandanchor.net. Tel. 831/649-6496. Monterey, 150 West Franklin.

Tutto Mondo Trattoria $

The mother/daughter team at this Italian eatery has created a very old and rustic ambiance in which to enjoy authentic Italian fare: hanging pots, wine bottles, worn tiled floors and textured walls. Open daily for lunch and dinner, recipes are pulled from momma's Italian-bred childhood. Pastas, sauces, pizzas, antipasti and desserts are all made on the premises. The wine list includes vintages from France, Italy and California. *Info:* www.mondos.com. Tel. 831-624.8977. Carmel, Delores St. between Ocean and Seventh.

Walnut Avenue Café $
Open for breakfast and lunch only, Walnut Avenue Café serves up some strong espresso concoctions, classic fare for breakfast and lunch, and some rather tasty omelets. The atmosphere is inviting and locals claim it's the best place for a morning meal. *Info:* www.walnutavenuecafe.com. Tel. 831/457-2307. Santa Cruz, 106 Walnut Ave.

TAHOE & YOSEMITE

LAKE TAHOE BEST SLEEPS
Black Bear Inn $$
Found adrift on a wooded acre overlooking Tahoe's mountainous beauty is this elegantly rustic inn that is less than a decade old. The public rooms at this adults-only inn feels like one of those great old lodges from another era with rough-hewn beams, heavy plank flooring and soaring ceiling. The river-rock fireplace is a welcoming centerpiece as is the elk's head that adorns it. There are a handful of rooms in the main lodge as well as a trio of cabins shaded by towering pines. Breakfast and evening wine included. *Info:* www.tahoeblackbear.com. Tel. 530/544-4451. South Lake Tahoe, 1202 Ski Run Blvd. 8 rooms/cabins.

Cottage Inn $$
This charming compound has a vintage vibe to it, and its location allows you to avoid the crowds. Built in the 1930s by the Pomin family, the inn features a scattering of multi-bedroom, knotty pine cottages as well as theme rooms, such as the Tahoe Teepee cloaked in a Native American motif. There is access to a private beach plus an outdoor hot tub, free breakfast and evening wine. Close to ski resorts and casinos. *Info:* www.thecottageinn.com. Tel. 530/581-4073. Tahoe City, 1690 West Lake Blvd. 14 rooms/cottages.

Tahoe-
Yosemite

Sutter Creek's Best!

Consider one of these for an overnighter in Sutter Creek:
- **The Foxes Inn**, www.foxesinn.com. Tel. 800/987-3344. 77 Main St. Just a half-dozen individually-appointed rooms tucked inside a Victorian home along the main drag.
- **Grey Gables Inn**, www.greygables.com. Tel. 209/267-1039. 161 Hanford St. An elegant English-style bed and breakfast located a few blocks from Main St.
- **Avio Vineyards & The Carriage House at Avio**, www.aviowine.com. Tel. 209/267-1515. 14520 Ridge Rd. Located just five minutes from downtown, this B&B (bed and bottle) is situated on the grounds of a winery and features a single and secluded guestroom. As a guest, you're privy to hike and picnic throughout the 30 acres of vineyards, pick ripe fruit from the tree to enjoy, learn how to make wine or prune the vines from the winemaker, or assist in the bottling process.

PlumpJack Squaw Valley Inn $$

Built as the home base for the 1960 Olympics, this stellar inn, owned in part by San Francisco mayor Gavin Newsom, features sophisticated rooms, excellent service, and a happening bar come sundown. The inn boasts a pool for summer travelers, and breakfast is included in the nightly rate. *Info:* www.plumpjack.com. Tel. 530/583-1576. Olympic Valley, 1920 Squaw Valley Road. 61 rooms/suites.

The Shore House at Lake Tahoe $$

The name clearly says it all. This lakefront inn, with its knotty-pine guest rooms, is a cozy find with misted waterviews, CD players, and rubber duckies holding court tubside.

A full breakfast is included, but you won't find a phone or television in site – which adds a certain tranquility we all yearn for while on holiday. *Info:* www.shorehouselaketahoe.com. Tel. 530/546-7270. Tahoe Vista, 7170 N. Lake Blvd. 9 rooms/cottages.

The Village at Squaw Valley USA $$
These one-, two- and three-bedroom condominiums were built in 2000. A home away from home at the base of the slopes, the modern, model-home feel of the individually-owned units include gas fireplaces, heated slate-tile floors, sleek kitchens, and living areas. Daily made service included. *Info:* www.thevillageatsquaw.com. Tel. 530/584-6205. Olympic Valley, 1985 Squaw Valley Rd. 290 units.

Rustic Cottage Resorts $
Clustered together near the lake, these simple and charming bungalows offer vintage beds, fireplaces and snug little porches. Reserve a single room or multiple rooms. Most have refrigerators and other conveniences, plus all have private baths. Breakfast is included. *Info:* www.rusticcottages.com. Tel. 530/546-3523. Tahoe Vista, 7449 N. Lake Blvd. 20 cottages.

LAKE TAHOE BEST EATS
Christy Hill $$$
There are few restaurants that can rival the views at this dinner-only restaurant. Situated just 100 feet above the shoreline on an elevated embankment, the a la carte menu is worth lingering over. The café menu, with its fish tacos, is less complicated but the starter and entrée listings — such as foie gras, Wild King Salmon, and flank steak — are impressive. Request a table outdoors when the weather calls for it. *Info:* www.christyhill.com. Tel. 530/583-8551. Tahoe City, 115 Grove St.

La Petit Pier $$$
Located lakefront with dreamy water views, this delightful dinner-only eatery offers a rich selection of food, from caviar to foie gras and lobster ravioli…and that's just for starters. Meals are a celebration of the palate and include

pheasant, Chilean sea bass and rack of lamb elegantly prepared and presented. *Info:* Tel. 530/546-4464. Tahoe Vista, 7238 North Lake Blvd.

Café Fiore $$

With only seven tables squeezed inside this charming cottage, you'll want to be sure to make a reservation. This very romantic bistro has a sophisticated Italian menu of pastas, veal entrees, and a catch — or two — of the day. Try the eggplant crepes, and don't skip the chance to savor the homemade, white chocolate ice cream. Heavenly! *Info:* www.cafefiore.com. Tel. 530/541-2980. South Lake Tahoe, 1169 Ski Run Blvd.

Freshies $$

This restaurant puts an emphasis on fresh, healthy food. The menu selection includes pulled pork sandwiches, excellent fish tacos, chicken sandwiches, and an incredible veggie tortilla soup, just to name a few. The strip mall setting leaves a bit to be desired, but if you can get past that you'll enjoy both the food and service. *Info:* Tel. 530/542-3630. South Lake Tahoe, 3300 Lake Tahoe Blvd.

Jake's on the Lake $$

This classic waterfront grill offers sweeping views of both the lake and surrounding mountains. The California cuisine offerings include a selection of fresh fish and seafood, steaks, soup, salads and a long list of appetizers. Lunch includes some creative sandwiches, and there is a kids menu too. *Info:* www.jakestahoe.com. Tel. 530/583-0188. Tahoe City, 780 North Lake Blvd.

Fire Sign Café $

If you want to find out where the good restaurants are, always look for the one with the queue. You'll never go wrong, and Fire Sign Café is proof of that. Open for bodacious breakfasts and hearty lunches, the locals love this place because the food is filling, delicious and cheap. Everything is made on the premises, and even the salmon is smoked here as well. A cup of Vienna-roasted coffee is just a $1. *Info:* Tel. 530/583-0871. Tahoe City, 1785 W. Lake Blvd.

YOSEMITE BEST SLEEPS

The Ahwahnee $$$

If you want to stay at The Ahwahnee, plan on making reservations months in advance. This unique and nostalgic lodge is a sentimental favorite. Boasting National Landmark status, the inn is known for its great granite façade, chunky beamed ceilings, soaring stone hearths, tapestry of Native American artwork and finely appointed rooms and cottages. Luxury service, such as nightly turndown and spa robes, create a refined ambiance among the rustic timber. *Info:* www.yosemitepark.com. Tel. 559.253-5635. Yosemite Village, Ahwahnee Rd. just north of Northside Dr. 127 rooms/suites/cottages.

Chateau du Sureau $$$

This European-style inn is certainly the most opulent to grace the Sierra Nevada. The spacious dwelling contains 10 rooms plus a separate two-bedroom villa that is ideal for large groups and families. Chambers are named for the abundance of herbs and flowers that punctuate the private estate and feature antique sleigh beds, fireplaces, sitting areas, enchanting views and all the amenities. The inn has its own award-winning restaurant where

cooking classes are hosted, plus a spa, swimming pool, and bocce court. The service is impeccable, and you won't find a front desk or check in area as guests are welcome by the innkeeper as if they're long lost friends. A handwritten summary of charges is discreetly presented at the end of your stay. *Info:*

www.elderberryhouse.com. Tel. 559/683-6860. Oakhurst, 48488 Victoria Ln. 11 rooms.

Homestead Cottages $
Built in 1992, these cozy one-bedroom cottages are an ideal alternative to camping because the experience is very rustic but

with added conveniences. There are just six abodes boasting natural pine wood-work, vaulted ceilings, tile floors and full-equipped kitchens. The Ranch House features two bedrooms and two bathrooms making it ideal for families. Kitchens in all cabins are stocked daily with coffee, tea, hot chocolate, milk, juice, muffins, fruit and granola. Gas barbecues and picnic tables are also available on the premises. While pets cannot be accommodated, those traveling with their horse can reserve a stable. *Info:* www.homesteadcottages.com. Tel. 559/683-0495. Ahwahnee, 41110 Rd 600. 6 cottages.

YOSEMITE BEST EATS
Erna's Elderberry House $$$
Located on the premises of Chateau du Sureau is this culinary treasure with its crimson walls, high ceilings and romantic aura. Seasonal six-course meals are paired with fabulous wines for an unforgettable dining experience. Complementing the setting is a stellar staff armed with old-school hospitality skills. *Info:* www.elderberryhouse.com. Tel. 559/683-6860. Oakhurst, 48488 Victoria Ln.

The Mountain Room Restaurant $$
What makes this restaurant a standout isn't so much the food, which is good, but the incredible views of the 2,424-foot high Yosemite Falls. With an emphasis on steaks, seafood and pasta, expect some tasty choices for dinner, from smoked trout cakes to duck confit and pasta – it's all good. *Info:* www.yosemitepark.com. Tel. 209/372-1274. Yosemite Village, at Yosemite Lodge at the Falls off Northside Dr.

THE NORTH COAST

BEST SLEEPS

Albion River Inn $$

Reminiscent of a New England village complete with rugged coastline, the selection of guest rooms and cottages all offer sweeping ocean and headland views. Choose your style of room, lovely to luxurious, and enjoy a full complimentary breakfast, wine upon arrival and in-room binoculars for seasonal whale watching. *Info:* www.albionriverinn.com. Tel. 707/937-1919. Albion, 3790 North Highway 1. 22 rooms/suites/cottages.

Glendeven Inn $$

Take refuge at this 19th-century estate overlooking Little River, just a few miles south of Mendocino Village. Guests are accommodated in either the farmhouse, carriage house or nearby annex where there are no televisions, phones or distractions. A hot breakfast is delivered to your room each morning, and wine and hors d'oeuvres are hosted each evening in the living room. *Info:* www.glendeven.com. Tel.707/937-0083- Little River, 8205 North Highway 1. 10 rooms/suites.

Stanford Inn by the Sea $$

The knotty pine walls and wood-burning fireplaces create a cozy setting behind guest room doors. The 11-acre inn, located just south of Mendocino Village, boasts a small working certified organic garden and farm that yields abundant fruits and vegetables. Each stay includes a full breakfast,  and there are kayaks and bikes for rent. Raven's Restaurant is here, which offers an array of entrees including vegan items. *Info:* www.stanfordinn.com. Tel. 707/937-5615. Mendocino, Coast Highway at Comptche Ukiah Rd. 33 rooms/suites.

Gingerbread Mansion $

Built at the turn of the 20th-century for a prominent Ferndale doctor is this lovely Victorian mansion with its handful of mostly ample-sized guest rooms and suites offering period-style furnishings and many original appointments. Included in each stay is a full gourmet breakfast, afternoon tea and evening wine service. *Info:* www.gingerbread-mansion.com. Tel. 707/786-4000. Ferndale, 400 Berding St. 11 rooms/suites.

Mendocino Hotel & Garden Suites $

If you're willing to walk across the hall to use the restroom, you can snag a room here for under $100; otherwise, those with private bathrooms at this historic Victorian charmer start at just $135. Built in 1878, this is Mendocino's only full-service hotel located in the heart of the village. Both modest and modernly-appointed luxury rooms are available in the main hotel and in the garden annex. *Info:* www.mendocinohotel.com. Tel. 707/937-0511- Mendocino, 45080 Main St. 51 rooms/suites.

The Victorian Village Inn $

Located near Ferndale's delightful village is this 1890 banker-built inn. Rooms are appointed in a style typical of the period. Full breakfast included, and fine dining and cocktails available at the inn's onsite restaurant. *Info:* www.victorianvillageinn.com. Tel. 707/786-4949. Ferndale, 400 Ocean Ave. 12 rooms.

BEST EATS
Café Beaujolais $$$

Located in a butter-colored Victorian bungalow, Café Beaujolais, like all other Mendocino restaurants, uses organically-grown products to create a tantalizing menu of fresh fish, duck and chops. Seasonal appetizers and desserts need some serious consideration, too. *Info:* www.cafebeaujolais.com. Tel. 707/937-5614. Mendocino, 961 Ukiah St.

Zebo $$$

The views at this restaurant are as tempting as its selection of fresh fish, GMO-free beef and poultry, and tidy wine list. Located on the grounds of the Elk Cove Inn, a few winding miles south of Mendocino, Zebo serves up a scrumptious dinner and divine scenery. *Info:* www.elkcoveinn.com. Tel. 707/877-3321. Elk, 6300 South Highway 1.

The Rendezvous $$$

Located on Main Street in Fort Bragg, this is one of Mendocino County's highly acclaimed restaurants. Housed in an historic 1897 home built for the town's apothecary, the restaurant is casually elegant with redwood paneling and a crackling fireplace. The dress code is also casual, but the menu is anything but pedestrian. The seasonal fare is a mélange of fresh pasta, steak, local seafood and a few gamey dishes. Summer brings wild king salmon, while the fall offerings might include boar or venison. The wine selection features mostly Mendocino and Anderson Valley varietals, and the beer selection includes some local brews as well. *Info:* www.rendezvousinn.com. Tel. 707/964-8142. Fort Bragg, 547 North Main St.

Curly's Grill $$

Located in the heart of downtown on the ground floor of the Victorian Inn is this local favorite serving fresh fish and pasta creations. Hearty breakfasts are available Sunday mornings, too. *Info:* Tel. 707/786-9696. Ferndale, 400 Ocean Ave.

Candy Stick Fountain & Grill $

Just the type of place you might expect to find in a town where time seems to stand still. Belly up to the soda fountain, sink your teeth into a juicy burger, or order a thick, gooey grilled cheese sandwich. There is also a jukebox, pool table, and nice big booths. *Info:* Tel. 707/786-9373. Ferndale, 361 Main St.

Lu's Kitchen $

This eatery is so tiny it hardly qualifies as a restaurant, but the selection of organic food mostly of the Mediterranean persuasion is certainly palate pleasing. There are a smattering of tables in the sheltered garden, which on most days requires a light jacket at minimum. You can also take the food to go. *Info:* Tel. 707/937-4939. Mendocino, 45013 Ukiah St.

10. BEST ACTIVITIES

This chapter is a quick reference and overview of some of Northern California's best vacation activities: **shopping, nightlife,** and year-round **sports and recreation.** You'll discover some fabulous shopping destinations, friendly bars, trendy nightclubs, relaxing places for a spa treatment, beautiful vineyards to go wine tasting, and suggestions for enjoying the great outdoors – including hiking, sun-bathing, water sports, skiing and much more.

SAN FRANCISCO

BEST SHOPPING

San Francisco is a bastion of boutiques, shops and hidden trea-
sures. In fact, even the so-called malls, such as the **Crocker
Galleria** and **Westfield San Francisco Center**, both near **Union
Square**, seem more like indoor metropolises.

Union Square, despite the crowds, is still a shopping destination
for many. You'll spot all the big names in and around the square:
Neiman Marcus, Bloomingdale's, Macy's, H&M, Nordstrom,
and **Sak's Fifth Avenue**. Specialty and designer stores, such as
Gump's, Sur La Table, Armani, Ralph Lauren, Frette, and a
three-story **Williams-Sonoma**, are also represented. Jutting off
Union Square is **Maiden Lane**, a concealed breezeway with
additional shops and galleries.

Most tourists never make their way to Cow Hollow's **Union
Street** (not to be confused with Union Square), located between
Steiner Street and Van Ness Avenue. It was the city's very first
neighborhood to convert its gingerbread Victorians into tony
boutiques, galleries and restaurants. While a few national retailers have managed to finagle their way in over the last few years,
the street remains lined with mostly individually-owned stores
and boutiques.

Chestnut Street, one block north of Lombard, in The Marina is
another hidden gem frequented mostly by locals. Its legion of
shops, eateries and coffee houses are mostly locally owned,
although you'll find Starbucks and a few other usual retail
suspects blending in with the scene. **Books Inc.** is a great place to
browse for titles and **The Humidor** is a must-stop for cigar
aficionados. Also, when hunger strikes, head to **Lucca Delicatessen** for a great Italian deli sandwich.

At the risk of sounding like a broken record, a trip to the **Ferry
Building Marketplace**, at the foot of Market along the
Embarcadero, is a must for anyone who enjoys food and food-

related products. You'll find rare antiques at **Culinaire**, artisan candles at **Mill Valley Candleworks**, and local epicurean delights from **Cowgirl Creamery**, **Acme Bread Company**, and the **Village Market**. There's also a great selection of eateries, plus a not-to-be-missed farmers market taking place outdoors Tuesday and Saturdays until 2pm.

Fillmore Street is another one of the city's great shopping destinations and one that tourists aren't likely to stumble upon. Surrounded by Japantown, Western Addition and Pacific Heights, this fun and funky shopping haven is located between Geary and Jackson. From independent booksellers, like **Juicy News**, to seductive lingerie draped about inside **Toujours**, a stroll along Fillmore Street makes for a delightful afternoon. There are also a number of resale shops where you can find real bargains.

Have a thing for Jesus action figures? Who doesn't. You can find these and more unusual wares, including punk and rockabilly clothing, at **Happy Trails** at Haight and Cole Streets. Retro lava lamps and other kitschy home décor is found at **Mickey's Monkey** at 214 Pierce Street. And, if you want the permanent San Francisco keepsake, stop in the **Soul Patch Tattoo** for a little skin inking or body piercing (henna tattoos are also available) at 1599 Haight Street.

Shopping Tip

If you want to avoid getting loaded down with bags full of cheap, touristy items, **steer clear of the shops around Fisherman's Wharf**. Sure, go ahead and look around. Poke through the racks of touristy t-shirts, sweatshirts and tote bags with images of the Golden Gate Bridge and other San Francisco landmarks, but avoid the urge to buy anything. The only store with any real merit is the culinary shop at Boudin's Bakery.

Within the **400 and 500 block of Castro Street** is where you'll find the charming **Cliff's Variety**, a hardware store that also hawks cookware, gifts, toys and games. **Does Your Father Know** has some rather naughty chatchkes. **Friendly Spirits** carries some 200 national and international wines, while **A Different Light Bookstore** stocks shelves of periodicals for gay and lesbian readers. For a slightly sexy bent — or for the fetish minded — check out **Worn Out West** for leather harnesses and jackets, police garb and fatigues. This store is not for the faint of heart. Over on nearby Market Street is where you'll find some great home shops, including mid-century modern musings at **Earthtones**. There's also a Pottery Barn on Market as well, but residents of The Castro tend to turn their noses up at what they consider an invasion of the national chain store.

In **Noe Valley**, get ready to shop up and down 24th Street between Church and Castro Streets. If you've been meaning to replace that avocado green fondue set from the '60s, then check out the **24th Street Cheese Company.** This tasty little find stocks fondue and raclette sets along with a selection of dipping companions, from breads and crackers to oils and olives. Break bread, along with scones, tarts and pies, at the **Noe Valley Bakery & Bread Company**, which is known for their artisan offerings. For the bibliophile **Cover to Cover** offers an array of books, including an impressive selection of travel-related guides; while **Phoenix Books** carries new and used books. The **SF Mystery Bookstore** at 4175 24th Street, offers both new and used whodunit scribes.

Across the Bay in Sausalito, the bulk of stores are located along Bridgeway. Aside from the art galleries, most tend to be very touristy. Except for a lone Starbucks, there really are no national retailers to be found around the waterfront. A couple of shops not to be missed include **Bacchus & Venus**. This wine gallery features tasting events, original art for sale, and items for the gourmand. *Info*: www.bacchusandvenus.com, Tel. 415/331-2001, 769 Bridgeway. I also like the **Pinestreet Papery** which carries imaginative stationery and gifts. It's located on a street that runs behind Bridgeway and is worth the few extra steps. *Info*: www.papery.com, Tel. 415/332-5458, 42 1/2 Caldonia.

BEST NIGHTLIFE
San Francisco's got an energetic and eclectic nightlife. You'll find the selection of after-hour haunts to be as multi-faceted as the city itself. There are high-energy dance clubs, intimate wine and jazz bars, karaoke bars, comedy clubs, and plenty of hotspots

San Francisco

catering to the gay and lesbian crowd. Expect to pay a cover charge at most dance clubs. Comedy clubs also have a cover charge and, typically, a two-drink minimum.

If you want to gyrate to hip hop on the dance floor, scour **SOMA** (short for South of Market Area) where converted warehouses conceal the trendiest clubs. Visiting celebrities are often spotted at **DNA Lounge** as well as the **Sound Factory**, with its young crowd and three floors of dancing. **Harlot** is an über cool VIP lounge featuring goth décor and hip DJs rivaled only by the nearby **Icon Ultra Lounge** and its unique glass bar.

The Mission district has some gritty bars and pubs that seem to appeal to rocker types or those whose closets are filled with worn jeans and Doc Martins. Throw back a beer at **Doctor Bombay's** (named for the character on the television show *Bewitched*) where you can order a drink by the name of Pixie Piss or visit **Jack's Elixir**, which has some 60 varieties of suds on tap.

If you like a more well-heeled crowed, check out the bars in **The Marina**, including **The Nectar Wine Lounge, Gravity** or the 20-seat **Bacchus Wine Bar**. **North Beach**, the city's Italian neighborhood, has some low-key clubs reminiscent of yesteryear's speakeasies, including **15 Romolo, Bimbo's 365 Club** where Rita Hayworth got her start and, for a laugh, **The Purple Onion** where Phyllis Diller and others have graced the stage.

No Smoking!

Care for a light? If so, better take it outside because the entire state of California forbids smoking in bars, restaurants, hotel lobbies, and public areas of any kind. Even some hotels, including guestrooms and suites, are completely smoke-free. Establishment owners will quickly enforce the code to avoid costly fines.

The Castro district is where you'll find the largest concentration of gay bars, although there are no specific women-only clubs. Notable watering holes in this area include **Detour, Harvey's**, and **Twin Peaks** for the 40-plus crowd.

A few landmark locations include the **Top of the Mark**, which crowns the **Mark Hop-**

Hopkins Hotel in Nob Hill. Unleashing a 1930s vibe is **Harry Denton's Starlight Room,** which sits atop the **Sir Francis Drake Hotel** in **Union Square.** And, one final favorite of mine, the **Buena Vista** near the **Fisherman Wharf** cable car turnaround at Hyde and Beach Streets. Belly up to the bar and enjoy an Irish Coffee, invented right here on the premises decades ago.

San Francisco

Over in Half Moon Bay, listen to live jazz at **Cetrella** downtown or retreat to the library inside the **Ritz-Carlton** for a nightcap and weekend jazz. The resort also has a new wine bar where you can sip your way around the world with its offering of international wines. **Huck Finn Sportfishing** also offers romantic night cruises if you're so inclined.

BEST SPORTS & RECREATION
Spectator Sports
Make no mistake about it; San Franciscans are fierce sports fans. You can tell because about every other person is wearing a Giants or Raiders cap, shirt, or sweatshirt. No matter what time of year you arrive, there is some professional sport being played on a field, rink, court or track in the Bay Area.

Baseball
The **San Francisco Giants** play right in the city at **AT&T Park** (*see photo at right*),

while the **Oakland Athletics,** also known as the Oakland A's, play in their city at **McAfee Coliseum,** the same stadium that the Oakland Raiders use during football season. The regular baseball season runs April-October. Both stadiums are easily accessible via public transportation. McAfee Stadium has a designated BART stop as well. *Info*: www.sfgiants.com; www.oaklandathletics.com.

Basketball

The Golden State Warriors play their season at the ORACLE Arena in Oakland from October-April. The Coliseum BART Station is just a short walk from the arena. Tickets are available online and at the box office. *Info*: www.nba.com/warriors.

Football

The **San Francisco 49ers** now play at **Monster Park** (formerly Candlestick Park), while the **Oakland Raiders** Play at **McAfee Coliseum** in Oakland. Pre-season games get underway in August with the regular season starting in September and continuing through December. *Info*: www.sf49ers.com; www.raiders.com.

Hockey

Neither San Francisco nor Oakland has a professional hockey team, so you'll have to drive to San Jose to get your puck-to-puck fix. The **San Jose Sharks**, part of the National Hockey League, play at HP Pavilion November through mid-April. *Info*: www.sj-sharks.com.

Horse Racing

The Bay Area offers two tracks where you can watch the ponies run. The first race of the day begins around 12:45pm and there are typically nine races a day with the eighth race being the stakes race. **Bay Meadows** is located south of the city in San Mateo (*see photo at*

left). The race season is February-May; and for two weeks during August. The Cal Train runs from San Francisco to the Hillsdale Station adjacent to the Bay Meadows parking lot. **Golden Gate Fields**, located in Berkeley, has a meet held during the months of January and February. *Info*: www.baymeadows.com; goldengatefields.com.

Participant Sports

Golf

You might be surprised to learn that you don't need to drive out of the city to tee off. The **Presidio Golf Course** is a superior 18-hole public course located about 10 minutes from downtown. **Golden Gate Park Golf Course** in Golden Gate Park is a par 3, nine-hole course set among cypress trees. And **Harding Park Golf Course** in the Sunset District is an 18-hole championship golf course with a nine-hole executive course offering practice areas and a full-service clubhouse. *Info*: presidiogolf.com; www.goldengateparkgolf.com; www.harding-park.com.

Biking & Walking

Golden Gate Park, with its many paved pathways, is an ideal place to safely walk or cycle in the city. Even inline skating is ideal here. There are seven miles of paved trails punctuated with waterfalls, lush gardens, and enjoyable scenery. More experienced cyclists may want to pedal across the **Golden Gate Bridge**, which will take you 1.7 miles across the bay and into the village of Sausalito where you can break for lunch and ride back to the city via the bridge or the ferry.

Day Spas

Many of the larger hotels have luxurious spas, including **The Huntington Hotel & Nob Hill Spa,** hence the name, atop Nob Hill. *Info*: www.huntingtonhotel.com. There are also some excellent, independent day spas including **Re:fresh**, one of the city's largest sanctuaries, located in the Financial District and offering 25-minute mini massages as well as 80-minutes of pampering. *Info*: www.refreshdayspa.com. For an authentic shiatsu massage stop into **Kabuki Springs and Spa** in Japantown (*see photo at right*) where you can soak in a traditional Japanese-style communal bath. *Info*: www.kabukisprings.com, Tel. 415/ 922-6000.

WINE COUNTRY: NAPA & SONOMA

BEST SHOPPING
The best shopping in The Wine Country is along the historic town squares in **Sonoma** and **Healdsburg**. **St. Helena, Petaluma, Napa**, and **Santa Rosa** all have charming downtown areas filled with individual shops stocked with gourmet foods, wine accessories, original artwork, and more.

The **Napa Premium Outlets**, off Highway 29 at the First Street exit, is filled with last season's goods from major designers and retailers. You'll find Barneys New York, J. Crew, Quicksilver, Gymboree, Cole Haan, Coach, Bose, and more. **Petaluma Village Premium Outlets** with its 60 retailers and charming hamlet setting, has many of the same designer and name brand stores. *Info*: www.premiumoutlets.com.

BEST NIGHTLIFE
The Wine Country isn't really known for its nightlife. Finding a place to sip pinot is simple; finding a place to party is almost impossible. There are a few late-night spots, including **étoile Wine Lounge at Domaine Chandon**. *Info*: www.chandon.com, Tel. 707/204-7529. Yountville, One California Drive.

BEST SPORTS & RECREATION
Golf
Your hotel concierge should be able to assist you with tee times at any one of the local courses. **Sonoma Fairmont Mission Inn** and the magnificent **Meadowood Napa Valley** both have award-winning golf courses, but you must be members or guests to use their facilities. *Info*: www.fairmont.com/sonoma; www.meadowood.com. **Windsor Country Golf**, located in Windsor near Santa Rosa in Sonoma County, is a lovely 18-hole course open to the public with fees under $40. *Info*: www.windsorgolf.com. **Silverado Resort** boasts two, 18-hole, Robert Trent Jones, Jr.-designed courses and non-guests are welcome. *Info*: www.silveradoresort.com.

Tennis
You would expect most full-service resorts to have tennis courts

for guests, but this proves not to be the case for Wine Country retreats. If you're set on playing tennis, check into **Meadowood Napa Valley** with its fleet of courts and resident tennis pro. *Info*: www.meadowood.com.

Wine Country

Hiking & Walking

Bothe-Napa Valley State Park offers great hiking near St. Helena. Fully developed on one side, and wild and rugged on the other, there are some 10 miles of hiking trails and 100 species of birds with occasional sightings of coyotes, bobcats and deer. *Info*: www.parks.ca.gov. Sonoma County has a lot of great parks for hiking, including **Sugarloaf Ridge State Park** (www. www.parks.ca.gov), **Spring Lake Regional Park** (www.sonomacounty.org/parks), and **Jack London Historic State Park** (www.parks.sonoma.net/JLPark.html). Sonoma's coastline also offers some nice hikes, including **Salmon Creek Beach** where a lagoon forms near the mouth of Salmon Creek. *Info*: www.parks.ca.gov.

Wine Tasting

The number of wineries and tasting rooms can be overwhelming. In Napa, do a little tasting off-the-beaten-path at **Chappellet Vineyard, Del Dotto**, and **Silverado Vineyards** (*see photo in sidebar*). *Info*: www.chappellet.com; www.deldottovineyards.com; www.silveradovineyards.com. In Sonoma, whet your palette at **Jordan Winery** in Healdsburg, the **Buena Vista Winery** near Sonoma, and **Clos**

Wine Tours

When it comes to wine tasting, leave the planning and driving to the experts at these tour companies:

- **Beau Wine Tours**, www.winetours.com, Tel. 707/938-8001
- **Classic Convertible Wine Tours**, www.antiquetours.net, Tel. 707/226-9227
- **California Wine Tours**, www.californiawinetours.com, Tel. 707/939-7225
- **Valley Wine Tours**, www.valleywinetours.com, Tel. 707/795-6462

du Bois in Geyserville. *Info*: www.jordanwinery.com; www.buenavistacarneros.com; www.closdubois.com.

Day Spas
Most full-service and boutique resorts house luxurious spas. Among the crème de la crème are **MacArthur Place** in Sonoma, **Kenwood Inn & Spa** in Kenwood, and Napa's **Meadowood Resort** in St. Helena. *Info*: www.macarthurplace.com; www.kenwoodinn.com; www.meadowood.com. The town of **Calistoga** in Napa Valley is known as the spa capital, and Lincoln Avenue, along with neighboring streets in downtown, has a number of simple to sublime spas to enjoy. **Dr. Wilkinson's Hot Springs Resort** is one of the oldest and more modest destinations. *Info*: www.drwilkinson.com.

Biking Tours
See the Wine Country on two wheels. **Wine Country Bike Tours** and **Napa Valley Bike Tours** take you down quiet country lanes and inside small family-owned wineries. *Info*: www.winecountrybikes.com; www.napavalleybiketours.com.

THE CENTRAL COAST

BEST SHOPPING
Each area of the Central Coast has its own shopping destinations where you can shop or browse through a number of quaint stores, boutiques and galleries.

Downtown Santa Cruz's streets are a mix of recognized retailers and individual shops, including places like **Chef Works** for aspiring culinary artists, **The Literary Guillotine** with its shelves of rare and used books, and **Ooh La La** for unique clothing. You'll also find the familiar with The Gap and Borders Books and Music, but these "found in every city" stores are outnumbered by the local proprietors.

Want to do some shopping in **Downtown Monterey**? You'll find some unique individual stores scattered throughout the area. **Del Monte Center**, located about two miles from the aquarium, is an open-air regional shopping center with a number of familiar names — Macys, Banana Republic, Pottery Barn, Williams-Sonoma — coupled with conveniences, such as a Whole Foods Market. *Info*: www.delmontecenter.com.

In **Carmel** you'll want to stroll along **Ocean Avenue** where a bevy of shops and art galleries are tucked inside Hansel & Gretel-style cottages. **Carmel Plaza**, at Ocean Avenue and Mission Street, is filled with mostly high-end shops and boutiques, such as Tiffany & Co., Louis Vuitton, and Cole Haan, plus some individual shops exclusive to Carmel.

Down south in **Cambria** you'll find a full range of specialty shops, art galleries and antique emporiums located mostly in the East Village area.

BEST NIGHTLIFE

For the most part, the Central Coast is like the Wine Country; nightlife just isn't the primary reason for choosing this as a travel destination. But, unlike Napa and Sonoma, you have more options. This is especially true of **Santa Cruz** where you'll find plenty of clubs and bars catering to all ages and tastes. **Catalyst** is the ultimate college hangout with its pulsating dance floor and music. *Info*: www.catalystclub.com. **The Blue Lagoon** hosts a weekly '80s Night while playing a mix of music the rest of the week.

Great Views & Food

Make the most of the coast at these top oceanfront/ocean view restaurants:
- **Cielo** at the Ventana Inn, www.ventanainn.com, Tel. 831/ 667-2331. Big Sur.
- **Pacific Edge Restaurant** at the Highlands Inn, www.highlandsinn.hyatt.com, Tel. 831/620-1234. Carmel.
- **The Terrace Lounge** at the Lodge at Pebble Beach, www.pebblebeach.com, Tel. 831/625-8524. Pebble Beach – 17 Mile Drive.
- **Old Fisherman's Grotto**, www.oldfishermansgrotto.com, Tel. 831/375-4604. Monterey.
- **The Hamlet at Moonstone Gardens**, www.moonstonegardens.com, Tel. 805/927-3535. Cambria.
- **Sea Chest Restaurant & Oyster Bar**, www.seachestrestaurant.com, Tel. 805/927-4514. Cambria

Central Coast

Info: www.thebluelagoon.com. The waterfront **Crow's Nest** has been entertaining folks since 1969 with its live music and laidback style. *Info*: www.crowsnest-santacruz.com.

Downtown Monterey, as well as **Cannery Row** (though this tends to be more touristy), has a number of nightclubs offering live music, such as **Cibo Ristoriante Italiano** with its line-up of live jazz and R&B music. *Info*: www.cibo.com. **The Crown & Anchor**, located below street level, really feels as if you've entered Central London with dark woods and a clientele of ex-patriots. *Info*: www.crownandanchor.net.

In **Carmel**, Terry's Bar at the charming **Cypress Inn**, owned by Doris Day, is a nice place for a drink with your doggie (yes, the actress is an animal activist and she extends her hospitality to pets). *Info*: www.cypress-inn.com. The lovely **Mission Ranch Inn** has a great piano bar frequented mostly by locals. *Info*: www.missionranchcarmel.com.

In **Cambria**, the choices quickly diminish. You'll find **Cambria Pines Lodge** has live music and dancing Friday and Saturday nights. *Info*: www.cambriapineslodge.com. **The Black Cat, An American Bistro and Wine Bar** is a nice escape once the sun goes down for a glass of wine and conversation. A little north at **San Simeon Beach Bar & Grill** you'll find live music, karaoke night, and great ocean views. *Info*: www.sansimeonrestaurant.com.

BEST SPORTS & RECREATION
Golf
Pasatiempo in Santa Cruz is one of the top three courses to play in California according to *Golf Digest*. This semi-private course is

very walkable since it was built prior to the use of electric carts. *Info*: www.pasatiempo.com. Without a doubt, the best golfing along the Central Coast, if not the continental United States, is **Pebble Beach** (*see photo at left*). Golfers have been flocking here since 1919, and the **Pebble Beach Golf Links** has been ranked the No. 1 Public Course in America by *Golf Digest*. The seascapes and fairways are breathtaking and, depending on what course you decide to play, rates can be as high as $500 for guests; $400 for resort guests. *Info*: www.pebblebeach.com. Some other pristine courses that are more affordable include **Poppy Hills Golf Course** in Pebble Beach and **Carmel Valley Ranch Golf Club** in Carmel. *Info*: www.poppyhillsgolf.com; www.cvrgolf.com.

Monterey is known as much for its natural beauty as it is for its manmade aesthetics: Golf courses. What golfer wouldn't want to conquer one of the pristine courses at the world-famous Pebble Beach Golf Links, home to the oldest, continuously operating golf course west of the Mississippi – **Del Monte Golf Course**. To do that, you'd better have a fat wallet, a tee time weeks—if not months—in advance, or a room reservation at one of the Pebble Beach resorts. If you have none of these, consider spending your Sunday golfing at one of the other 20 private and public courses. *Info*: To help with planning a day on the golf course, visit **Monterey County Golf Guide** at www.golfmonterey.org. Here you can request a free course guide, schedule a tee time, preview a golfing getaway, and more.

Hiking & Walking

Henry Cowell Redwoods State Park, located in Felton, part of Santa Cruz County, features 15 miles of hiking trails through a thick forest that has changed little in the last two centuries. The park's Redwood Grove features a self-guided nature path punctuated with Douglas fir, madrone, oak and a thatch of Ponderosa Pine. The oldest trees in the park are more than 1400 years old. You can pack a lunch and enjoy an impromptu picnic under one of these soaring treasures. *Info*: www.santacruzstateparks.org/parks/henrycowell.

Point Lobos State Reserve, just south of **Carmel,** has seven miles of rugged trails for roaming, while 541-acre **Garland Ranch Regional Park** in **Carmel Valley** near the Carmel River offers some dramatic scenic views for those on foot. *Info:* pt-lobos.parks.state.ca.us; www.carmelvalley.com.

Near Cambria, on the northside of Highway 1 near San Simeon Creek Bridge, is **San Simeon State Park.** At the end of the boardwalk is an excellent trail that continues south across the wetlands and up into the towering forest of pine trees. It's a peaceful, leisurely three-mile hike. *Info:* www.cambriachamber.org/hiking.php.

Horseback Riding
Gallup along the beach in **Big Sur, Moss Landing** or **Pebble Beach** with **Monterey Tours,** which offers one-hour seaside rides. *Info:* www.montereytours.com. **Molera Horseback Tours** offers rides exclusively in **Andrew Molera State Park** in Big Sur where you can trot over flower-studded meadows, past soaring Redwood groves, and along crystal clear streams and secluded beaches. *Info:* www.molerahorsebacktours.com.

Skateboarding
In **Santa Cruz,** skateboarders can really go to town at **Ken Wormhoudt Skate Park.** *Info:* www.socalskateparks.com/park/santacruz. Open daily from 9am to sunset; helmets elbow pads and knee pads required. **El Estero Park** in **Monterey,** located next to the Dennis the Menace Playground, offers skateboarders their very own sanctuary with 8,000 square feet of ledges, half-pipes, and ramps. *Info:* www.monterey.org/rec/locations.html.

Biking
The seven-mile bayside **Monterey Peninsula Recreational Trail** is ideal for cyclists and skaters with its smooth pavement and scenery. For a more challenging pedal, head to the rougher trails of **Fort Ord,** the former U.S. Army post that is now part of the U.S. Bureau of Land Management.

Surfing
The best and safest beaches to surf are those in Santa Cruz.

Central
Coast

Pleasure Point Beach is a popular haunt for surfers and is open sunrise to sunset.

Wine Tasting

Santa Cruz, Monterey and San Luis Obispo Counties all boast their own wine regions and varietals. Spend an afternoon in each region exploring the wine trails and tasting rooms. You can download **wine trail maps** for each area at: www.scmwa.com; www.montereywines.org; www.pasowine.com .

Day Spas

Along the Monterey Peninsula, the best spas are those found inside posh resorts. **The Spa at Pebble Beach** is a haven for hedonistic treatments with facials, wraps and aromatherapy. *Info*: www.pebblebeach.com. The spa at **Post Ranch Inn** is equally incredible (*see photo below*) though more rustic than Pebble Beach, with its signature Big Sur Jade Stone Therapy treatment featuring basalt river rocks combined with massage. *Info*: www.postranchinn.com.

Water Safety

Every year people drown along the California coast simply because they're unaware of the dangers and how powerful the ocean can be. Here are some tips to stay safe:

• **Never dive head-first** into the surf even if you're familiar with the terrain. You could easily hit hidden rocks or the shallow bottom resulting in permanent paralysis or death.

• **Beware of rip currents**, which are swift flows of backwash that surge through the surf. If caught in these riptides, do not swim against the current; instead, swim parallel to the beach until free of the strong tide and then head to shore. Early breaking waves and choppy, foamy or discolored water are signs of such danger zones.

• Always keep an eye on the surf and young children away from the foam line because **sleeper waves** can hit the shore without warning. These enormous waves crash much farther up the beach than a normal wave, and they can send kids and adults tumbling to the ground before dragging them into the deep water.

TAHOE & YOSEMITE

BEST SHOPPING

Head to **Incline Village** and its **Christmas Tree Village**, which is filled with souvenir shops, a home décor store and restaurants. At **Northstar-At-Tahoe** they have a shopping village filled with high-end clothing stores and galleries. Along North Lake Boulevard in **Tahoe City** is a fleet of shoreline stores, restaurants and boutiques. The shops at the **Resort at Squaw Creek** contains an indoor and outdoor area filled with galleries, sporting shops, and clothing stores. **Downtown Truckee** is the most authentic shopping area because it's a true, historic walking town with bookstores, clothing boutiques, and convenient services. The **Village at Squaw Valley** resembles a European-style pedestrian village with many high-end shops. *Info*: www.squawcreek.com; www.villageatsquaw.com; www.historictruckee.com.

BEST NIGHTLIFE

Stargazing is about your only option after dark in Yosemite, but you can stay up all night at one of Lake Tahoe's casinos located on the Nevada side. **Harrah's** and **Cal-Neva Resort**, whose storied history includes Frank Sinatra's brief stint as an owner, are stock piled with slot machines, roulette and black jack tables, and entertainment. *Info*: www.harrahs.com; www.calnevaresort.com.

BEST SPORTS & RECREATION
Adventure

A hot-air balloon ride over Lake Tahoe takes some finessing

to launch. **The Tahoe Flyer**, a 21 ton, two-deck, catamaran-style aircraft carrier vessel designed and built to inflate and launch hot-air balloons, is where the adventure starts. At the end of the flight, participants join the crew in a

Champagne toast and a round of mimosas. *Info*: www.laketahoeballoons.com. Over in Yosemite, climbing **Half Dome** is the most thrilling experience, but the 17-mile, round-trip trek takes stamina and experience.

Tahoe-Yosemite

Skiing/Snowboarding
Lake Tahoe has lots of great places to ski, among the best are **Heavenly Resort, Alpine Meadows** and **Squaw Valley**. Skiers and snowboarders can do a little mogul jumping at Yosemite's **Badger Pass**. *Info*: www.skiheavenly.com; www.alpinemeadows.com; www.squaw.com; www.yosemitepark.com.

Hiking
A hike to the base of **Bridalveil Fall** in **Yosemite** takes you to the base of a lovely waterfall. **Lower Yosemite Fall Trailhead** is also a nice hike that takes about 30 minutes and is appropriate for all skill levels. Because the waterfalls in Yosemite are mostly snow fed, they gush in the spring and early summer but are typically dry from late July to October. The ultimate Yosemite hiking experience is, of course, **Half Dome.**

Easy Yosemite Trails

Yosemite's best hiking trails for beginners are:
- **Bridalveil Fall**
- **Lower Yosemite Fall**
- **Cook's Meadow Loop**
- **Mirror Lake/Meadow**

Horseback Riding
A guided horseback ride through **Yosemite** can be a peaceful way to enjoy the park's beauty. Several companies offer guided rides, including **Minarets Pack Station** which leads day trips to Yosemite and the Ansel Adams Wilderness. *Info*: www.highsierrapackers.org.

Biking & Walking
You'll find plenty of biking and walking trails in and around **Lake Tahoe**. The most scenic, and perhaps flattest option, is

around the entire lake which, from start to finish, is 72 miles. You have the option to go the whole nine yards or just do a section. The only steep grade is from Carnelian Bay to the top of Dollar Hill. Lake Tahoe has an endless supply of places to pedal, from trails to paved pathways. **Olympic Bike Shop** in Tahoe City offers one-stop service for rentals, repairs and clothing. *Info*: Tel. 530/581-2500. The staff can also help you chart your course.

Mountain Biking

If you enjoy mountain biking, try blazing a trail or two on these top Tahoe paths:
• **Emigrant Trail** in Truckee
• **Flume Trail** in Incline Village
• **Tahoe Rim Trail** from Truckee to InclineVillage
• **Mr. Toad's Wild Ride**, Incline Village to Myers
• **Angora Ridge**, from Tahoe City to Fallen Leaf Lake Road

Boating
There are plenty of tour operators offering scenic boat and yacht cruises on the lake. If you don't believe me, just ask the hotel concierge. However, **Tahoe Thunder** offers the ultimate adrenaline ride aboard Tahoe's fastest speed boat. The hair-raising experience takes you to Emerald Bay from Timbercove Marina. *Info:* Tel. 530/541-7245. South Lake Tahoe. 4311 Lake Tahoe Boulevard.

River Rafting
You won't make much headway with a raft on the lake, but motor on over to the **Truckee River**, the lake's one and only outlet, and you can enjoy a gentle but exciting ride down the waterway. The 2-3 hour, five-mile float takes you from **Tahoe City** to the **River Ranch Lodge**. A free shuttle bus will bring you back to your car once the ride is over. While you're waiting why not reward yourself—after all, you made it in one piece—with an ice-cold beer on the riverfront deck of the lodge. Make it two…shuttles do run frequently, so there's always another on its way. *Info:* www.truckeeriverraft.com. Tel. 530/583-0123. Tahoe City. 185 River Road. $32 adults, $27 children. Open June through September.

Scuba Diving

Lake Tahoe's **Emerald Bay** is a designated underwater state park and a resting place for countless boats, launches and barges that have been submerged for decades. Aside from abandoned watercraft, there are also several trees that are thousands of years old thriving below the water's surface. *Info:* www.parks.ca.gov.

Day Spas

An après ski massage seems like a logical choice after a day on the slopes. Book and appointment at the **Resort at Squaw Creek** or **Cal Neva Resort,** or enjoy a less expensive treatment at **Lighthouse Massage Therapy** overlooking the lake. Therapists will also bring the spa experience to you. *Info:* www.squawcreek.com; www.calnevaresort.com; www.lighthousespa.com.

THE NORTH COAST

BEST SHOPPING

The villages of **Mendocino** and **Ferndale,** along with **Eureka's Old Town**, have a fleet of unique shops and galleries. You'll find new books and those with tattered covers, clothes, art, home furnishings and more.

BEST SPORTS & RECREATION

Boat Tours

A two-hour narrated boat tour conducted by Camp Weott Guide Services takes you along the **Eel River Estuary** near Ferndale where you'll encounter local wildlife while making your way down the river towards the Pacific Ocean. *Info:* Tel. 707/786-4187.

Kayaking & Canoeing

The **Big River Estuary** lets you paddle through the forested canyon while working with the weather and tides. Ideal for both the novice and the pro; although, trips against the tide can be more challenging. Van Damme State Beach, a few miles south of Mendocino on Highway 1, is another popular spot for kayaking. Rentals are available at **Stanford Inn by the Sea**. *Info:* www.stanfordinn.com. Tel. 707/937-5615. **Lost Coast Kayaking** also offers guided tours into sea caves. Up in Eureka, **Woodley**

Island Marina is a great place for kayaking. **Hum Boats** offers group lessons on the bay, lagoons, lakes or estuaries. *Info:* www.lostcoastkayaking.com; www.humboats.com.

Bird Watching
Russ Park in Ferndale boasts a 110-acre, closed-canopy bird sanctuary with three miles of hiking trails.

Scenic Drive
The **Avenue of the Giants**, which skirts the Eel River through the amazing Humboldt Redwoods State Park, is one of the most breath-taking routes in all the West. *Info:* www.avenueofthegiants.net.

Hiking
Russian Gulch State Park, which fronts the ocean near Mendocino, is ideal for exploring and hiking. There's beaches and tide pools plus sea caves and a 36-foot-high waterfall. *Info:* www.parks.ca.gov.

Wine Tasting
Take **Highway 128** through the **Anderson Valley** for an excellent wine tasting experience. The planted acreage in the Anderson Valley consists primarily of Pinot Noir, Chardonnay, Gewürztraminer and White Riesling. There are also small acre-ages of other varietals such as Sauvignon Blanc, Pinot Gris, Cabernet Sauvignon and Zinfandel.

Horseback Riding
Ricochet Ridge Ranch in Mendocino County guides those on horseback along Ten Mile Beach and through the Redwood Forest on a most serene ride. *Info:* Tel. 888/873-5777. **Redwood Trails** along the Lost Coast, between Eureka and Crescent City, is surrounded by greenbelts, lagoons and the Pacific Ocean. Horse rentals are available on-site. *Info:* Tel. 707/488-2061.

Biking & Walking

Mendocino offers hundreds of miles of back roads, abandoned logging roads and trails for hiking and mountain biking – even leisurely walks. Maps and bike rentals are available at Stanford Inn-by-the-Sea. **Russian Gulch State Park** is perfect for exploring and hiking. The park features 1,162 acres with 7,630 feet of ocean frontage replete with rugged headlands, beaches and tide pools. One side is the Devil's Punch Bowl sea cave, on the other is the forested Russian Gulch Creek Canyon and the 36-foot high waterfall.

North Coast

Day Spas

Both the **Inn at Schoolhouse Creek** and the **Stanford Inn By-the-Sea** have relaxing spas for massage, body treatments and facials. Don't feel like leaving your room, but still need a little kneading? The team from Body Works comes to you with their "spa on the go." *Info:* www.schoolhousecreek.com; www.stanfordinn.com.

11. PRACTICAL MATTERS

AIRPORTS/ARRIVALS

Northern California is served by four major airports along with a handful of regional airports. There are taxis, shuttle services, hotel courtesy vans, and public buses located at all the airport terminals as you exit the baggage claim area – in most cases there are marked signs where these vehicles are allowed to stop. Except for San Francisco International Airport (SFO), Oakland International Airport (OAK), and San Jose International Airport (SJC), all of the other airports serving Northern California have car rental companies located on-site. SFO, OAK, and SJC have a single **Rental Car Center** that houses several major rental car companies a few miles from their airport terminal. The rental car companies are allowed to pick up and drop off their guests directly from the airline terminals using courtesy shuttle vans.

The San Francisco Bay Area is served by **San Francisco International Airport** (SFO), located south of the city, which is the world's 30th busiest airport. Touted as the "gateway to the Pacific," SFO is home to more than 40 national and international airline carriers. Getting in and out of the airport to the city is easy using public transportation, including **Bay Area Rapid Transit** (BART). Taxis, of course, are plentiful and finding someone to share a ride into San Francisco is usually not a problem. *Info*: www.flysfo.com. Tel. 800/435-9736. The airport is visible from Highway 101 and is located off the San Francisco International Airport exit 13 miles south of the city near the Highway 380 junction.

Latest Traffic Info

For the most **current traffic information** for the San Francisco Bay Area, visit **www.transit511.org** or call 511 from within the Bay Area (or 510/817-1717 from outside the Bay Area).

Oakland International Airport (OAK) is a medium-sized hub and full-service airport that also serves the San Francisco Bay Area with 15 mostly national airline carriers. OAK is an ideal choice if you're bypassing San Francisco and heading straight to Napa Valley or Berkeley. Since it's less congested than SFO, many people prefer to fly into OAK and motor across the Bay Bridge into San Francisco. The airport is served by Alaska Airlines, Horizon Air, American Airlines, Continental Airlines, Delta Airlines, Delta Connection, JetBlue, Mexicana, Skybus, Southwest Airlines, United Airlines, United Express, and US Airways. Both SFO and OAK are the closet major airports to California's Northern Coast. *Info*: www.oaklandairport.com. Oakland, 1 Airport Dr.

If you plan on beginning or ending your trip in Santa Cruz or the Monterey Bay Peninsula, then you'll want to fly into **San Jose International Airport** (SJC). Located about an hour from San Francisco via car and just minutes from downtown San Jose, the airport is serviced by Alaska Airlines, American Airlines/American Eagle, Continental Airlines, Delta Airlines, Frontier Airlines, Hawaiian Airlines, Horizon Air, JetBlue, Mexicana, Northwest Airlines, Southwest Airlines, United Airlines, United Express, and US Airways. *Info*: www.sjc.org. Tel. 408/501-0979. San Jose, 2077 Airport Blvd.

Sacramento International Airport (SMF) is located 12 miles outside of the state capital and is the closest major airport to **Lake Tahoe**. It's also an alternative airport if you're visiting the Wine Country. The airport is serviced by 17 airline carriers: Air Canada, Alaska Airlines, American Airlines, Continental Airlines, Delta Airlines, ExpressJet, Frontier Airlines, Hawaiian Airlines, Horizon Air, JetBlue, Mexicana, Northwest Airlines, Southwest Airlines, United Airlines, United Express, and US Airways. *Info*: www.sacairports.org. Tel. 916/929-5411. Sacramento, 6900 Airport Blvd.

Northern California also has several small, municipal airports that offer connecting flights from some of the area's larger airports. Many of these airports, which are listed below, also offer non-stop service to and from various parts of the country.

The **Arcata-Eureka Airport** (ACV) is located in Humboldt County, also known as California's Lost Coast. This regional airport provides limited commercial air service to and from Humboldt, Del Norte and Mendocino Counties. It is currently served by two commercial airlines, Horizon Air, which provides service to and from Seattle, Portland and Redding, California; and United Airlines. You can catch connecting flights on United from San Francisco or Sacramento, as well as direct service from Portland, Oregon, if you're planning on visiting Ferndale or the Mendocino Coast. *Info*: Tel. 707/445-7491. McKinleyville, 3561 Boeing Ave.

Charles M. Shultz Sonoma County Airport, named in honor of the Peanuts comic strip creator, is located 65 miles north of San Francisco and 50 miles west of Napa in Santa Rosa, where Shultz lived and worked for more than 30 years. At present, only Horizon Air provides nonstop service to and from Los Angeles, Portland and Seattle. If you're plan on visiting the Wine Country and North Coast, and can arrange for a connecting flight from Los Angeles or Seattle, this would be a convenient alternative to the major Bay Area airports. *Info*: www.sonomacountyairport.com. Tel. 707/565-7243. Santa Rosa, 2290 Airport Blvd.

Fresno Yosemite International Airport (FYI), located in central California, is about 2 1/2 hours from Yosemite National Park. The airport is serviced by Alaska Airlines, Allegiant Airlines, U.S. Airways, American/American Eagle, Continental Airlines, Delta Airlines/Skywest, ExpressJet, Hawaiian Airlines, Horizon Air, Mexicana Airlines, Northwest Airlines, United/United West Airlines. *Info*: www.flyfresno.org. Tel. 559/621-4500. Fresno, 4995 E. Clinton Way.

The **Monterey Peninsula Airport** (MYR) offers flights to and from San Francisco, Los Angeles, Phoenix, Denver, Las Vegas, Salt Lake City, and San Diego. This small and convenient airport is ideal if you're planning on traveling from the Monterey Bay Peninsula down Highway 1 to such coastal destinations as Big Sur and Hearst Castle in San Simeon. There are just five air carriers, including American Eagle with non-stop service to Los Angeles; Delta Airlines with non-stop service to Salt Lake City; ExpressJet with service to Eastern Los Angeles and San Diego;

United Airlines and United Express with non-stop service to Los Angeles, San Francisco and Denver; and U.S. Airways with non-stop service to Phoenix and Las Vegas. *Info*: www.montereyairport.com. Tel. 831/648-7000. Monterey, 200 Fred Kane Dr.

Reno-Tahoe International Airport (RNO) is actually located in Nevada, but just a short distance from Lake Tahoe, California. It is served by Alaska Airlines, Horizon Air, American Airlines, Continental Airlines, Delta Airlines, Delta Connection, Frontier Airlines, Southwest Airlines, United Airlines, and U.S. Airways. *Info*: www.renoairport.com, Tel. 775/328-6870. Reno, 2001 E. Plum Ln.

Santa Barbara Airport (SBA), located north of Downtown Santa Barbara, would be the closest and most convenient airport if you were beginning or ending your trip with a visit to Hearst Castle in San Simeon. The airport offers non-stop service to and from Dallas/Ft. Worth, Denver, Las Vegas, Los Angeles, Phoenix, Portland, Salt Lake City, San Francisco, San Jose, and Seattle. Six commercial airlines service SBA, including Alaska, American/ American Eagle, Delta Connection, Horizon Air, United Express, and US Airways. *Info*: www.flysba.com. Tel. 805.681.4804. Santa Barbara, 500 Fowler Rd.

GETTING AROUND
By Air
It is possible to destination hop via air travel through Northern California, though I don't recommend it. First of all, many of the highways, byways and two-lane roads meander past some spectacular landscapes that can only be enjoyed on the ground. Also, service is limited and sporadic at best.

The furthest point, from Cambria proper to Ferndale (there are no direct flights between the two cities as neither place has commercial air service), follows the coast for a good chunk of the way and will take you approximately 8 hours by car without traffic – but few embark on such an ambitious drive in a single day.

Another reason I don't recommend inter-regional air travel throughout Northern California is because of the hassle in our post 9/11 world. It will rarely save you time as all airlines require you to check-in at least two hours prior to your flight and, depending on where you are departing from and arriving to, it's very likely you'll encounter freeway congestion (allow for travel time to the airport), airport congestion, long lines at the check-in counter, security checks, a wait at baggage claim, and possible delays in taking off and/or landing. By the time you add all of these factors into the mix, you could have likely reached your destination while the plane is still en route.

By Bus
Greyhound provides inter-city bus service throughout much of Northern California. The one unique trait about going Greyhound is that the bus often travels the back roads, stopping in the smaller communities en route to the big cities. The downside is that it takes much longer to reach your destination. *Info*: www.greyhound.com. Tel. 800/231-2222.

By Car
The best and most convenient way to travel Northern California is by car. Without a car it's likely you won't be able to take advantage of all there is to do and see. Most heavy traffic conditions, five-lane highways, and freeway interchanges take place in and around San Francisco and Oakland. Other areas, such as the Silicon Valley (San Jose area), can also experience heavy congestion during peak hours. However, the roads leading to the more bucolic regions, such as the Wine Country, North and Lost Coast, and along Highway 1 are picture perfect with mild congestion. Driving maps of Northern California are available from AAA and at the desks of most car rental companies. Many rental car agencies also offer Global Positioning Systems (GPS) at an additional charge.

By Train
Train travel in Northern California can be very scenic. Amtrak has various routes that run through the region and state. The **California Zephyr** originates in Emeryville near San Francisco and concludes in Chicago with stops to Sacramento, Reno near Lake Tahoe and several other destinations along the way. The **Capitol Corridor** begins in San Jose and travels eastbound through

the state all the way to Auburn with stops to such major destinations as Oakland and Sacramento. The **Coast Starlight** travels between Los Angeles (Union Station) and Santa Barbara before heading up the coast to its final destination in Seattle stopping in a few Central Coast and Northern California cities, including San Luis Obispo, San Jose and Sacramento, just to name a few. Finally, you can take the **San Joaquins** from Oakland to Sacramento. *Info*: www.amtrak.com. Tel. 800/872-7245.

By Taxi
For the most part, you won't have a problem hailing a cab in San Francisco. They are literally everywhere. Outside the city is a different matter. Napa Valley has limited taxi service, so have your hotel concierge or restaurant host call ahead for you. Sonoma has even fewer options with Vern's Taxi Service (Tel. 707/938-8885) being just about the only gig in town. Still, if you need a designated driver don't hesitate to call. Carmel, Monterey and Santa Cruz all have taxi sightings, but again service is limited. As for Mendocino and Ferndale, taxi service is almost non-existent.

By Public Transportation
Public transportation within San Francisco is, in my opinion, phenomenal. Rarely do I bother driving while in the city since buses, cable cars and taxis are readily available night and day. Aside from San Francisco, Northern California's other regions also have public transportation with some having more limited options than others. Contact the following for routes, timetables and general information:
• **San Francisco Municipal Transportation Agency**, www.sfmta.com. Tel. 415/701-4500.
• **San Francisco Bay Area Rapid Transit District**, www.bart.gov. Tel. 415/989-2278

- **Sonoma County Transit**, www.sctransit.com, Tel. 707/576-7433
- **The Vine, Napa County Transportation & Planning Agency**, Tel. 707/252-2600
- **Mendocino Transit Authority**, www.4mta.org, Tel. 707/462-1422
- **Monterey-Salinas Transit** (includes Carmel), www.mst.org, Tel. 888/678-2871
- **Santa Cruz Metropolitan Transit District**, www.scmtd.com, Tel. 831/425-8600
- **Tahoe Area Regional Transit**, www.placer.ca.gov, Tel. 530/550-1212
- **Yosemite Area Regional Transit System**, www.yarts.com, Tel. 877/989-2787

BASIC INFORMATION
Business Hours
These hours vary greatly depending on how you define "business." Services, such as dry cleaners and automotive repair shops, generally operate a standard 9-to-5 day Monday-Saturday. Retail stores and shopping malls are generally open seven days a week 10am-9pm Monday-Friday, until 7pm on Saturday, and from 11am-6pm on Sunday. Many major grocery stores and pharmacy chains, such as CVB, Walgreens and Rite-Aid, are open 24 hours. Cultural venues, such as museums, are often closed Monday and Tuesday so call ahead for hours.

Climate & Weather
Travel to San Francisco and the Northern California region, including the Central Coast, is enjoyable year round. Believe it or not, **San Francisco can be extremely chilly during the summer months** – pack long pants and a jacket. Most people travel to the state mid-June to late August, which makes attractions, such as Yosemite, unbelievably crowded. Nightly rates at hotels and inns are also at their highest. Fall is a great time to visit Northern California and the Wine Country, and it's the time of year when San Francisco enjoys its sunniest days. Lake Tahoe is both a summer and winter destination. Skiers can expect snow as early as late October, but conditions improve greatly later in the season. Expect long lift lines on holidays and weekends.

Driving Laws & Tips

Follow these rules of the road if you do not want to get a ticket! For additional driving laws and safety tips, visit the California DMV website at www.dmv.ca.gov.

- You must carry a valid driver's license from your home state or country.
- The minimum age for drivers is 16 with training, 18 without.
- California right allows motorists to make a right-hand turn after coming to a complete stop at a red light. Conditions must be safe, and there can be no signs prohibiting the maneuver.
- Call boxes are located every quarter mile on the freeway, and operators can connect you to the Auto Club, family members or your insurance company. Face traffic, and be aware of on-coming vehicles.
- Freeway carpool lanes, usually marked with a diamond sym-bol, and metered on-ramps are generally open to any vehicle with more than a solo driver. Pay attention, as there are few exceptions.
- Children under six years or less than 60 pounds must be in an approved safety car seat while vehicles are in motion.
- All passengers must wear seat belts at all times when a car is moving.
- It's now against the law to drive and talk on a cell phone unless using a hands-free device.

Electricity

The standard electrical current for Northern California, as well as the entire U.S., is 110 volts.

Emergencies & Safety

In life-threatening situations, emergency assistance for police, fire or medical needs is 911, which is a toll-free telephone call from any public phone. You may be required to dial a "9" first from a hotel room, or you can press zero and ask the hotel operator to assist you.

Be sure to take precautions as you would anywhere else. Don't leave expensive electronic devices or handbags on the front seat of your car and lock your car when you enter and exit your vehicle. One precaution I always use as a hotel guest is to hang the "do not disturb" sign on the outside of my door once my room has been serviced and I'm leaving for the day. It makes it appear as if someone is in the room. Another safety precaution is to never open your hotel room door without first looking through the peephole.

Festivals & Holidays

Northern California, like the rest of the state, observes all national holidays. Some notable events that take place throughout the year include the:
- **Cambria Art & Wine Festival** during the last weekend in January
- **Napa Valley Mustard Festival** in January

- **Chinese New Year Festival & Parade** in San Francisco during February
- **Sonoma Valley Olive Festival** finale in February
- **Clam Chowder Cook-Off** on the Santa Cruz Pier in February
- San Francisco's **Cherry Blossom Festival of Northern California** in April
- **Carmel Art Festival** in May
- Monterey County's annual **Steinbeck Festival** in August
- **Yosemite Facelift** in September
- **Fleet Week** in **San Francisco** during October
- **Mendocino Mushroom Madness** starts in November with a plethora of events throughout the fall and winter months
- Monterey's **Christmas in the Adobes** in December
- **Holiday Bed and Breakfast Tour** in and around Napa in early December
- Ferndale's **Christmas Lighted Tractor Parade** in mid December

Liquor Laws

The legal age for purchase and consumption of alcoholic beverages is 21; proof of age is required. Liquor, grocer, and some drug stores sell packaged alcohol daily from 6am to 2am. Most restaurants, bars and nightclubs are licensed to serve a full line of beverages during the same hours. Some restaurants are only permitted to sell beer and wine.

Freeway System

Northern California's freeway system, for the most part, is relatively simple to maneuver. The San Francisco Bay Area boasts an extensive and somewhat confusing network consisting of mostly interstate highways. Since San Francisco is considered Northern California's major metropolis, the following freeways will connect you from the city to other parts of the region.

Take these roads for destinations north of San Francisco:
• **Sacramento** – Interstate 80
• **Napa/Sonoma** – Route 12 via Highway 101 north
• **Mendocino Coast** – Route 128 via Highway 101 north
• **Ferndale/Northern Coast** – Route 211 via Highway 101 north
• **Lake Tahoe** – Highway 50 via Interstate 80

Take these roads for destinations south of San Francisco:
• **San Jose** – Highway 101 south or Interstate 280 (the more scenic and less traveled route)
• **Santa Cruz** – Route 17 via Highway 101 south

Regional Lingo

The Bay Area is broken into regions, and locals have their own lingo when it comes to geography.
• San Francisco is simply known as "**The City.**"
• **The East Bay**, which lies across the water from The City, includes Contra Costa and Alameda Counties, home to Oakland and Berkeley.
• Santa Clara County and the city of San Jose are considered **the South Bay**.
• **The Peninsula**, which stretches from San Francisco all the way across San Mateo County reaching into Santa Clara County includes a number of destinations, such as Palo Alto, home of Stanford University, Half Moon Bay, and South San Francisco, to name a few.

- **Monterey Bay Peninsula/Carmel** – Route 68 via Highway 101 south
- **Cambria/Hearst Castle** – Route 46 via Highway 101 south
- **Yosemite National Park** – Route 120 east or 140 east via Interstate 580

To reach Santa Cruz, Monterey Bay Peninsula or Cambria/ Hearst Castle, you can take the more scenic route using Highway 1. It's a gorgeous drive albeit treacherous at times and much slower than if you were to take Highway 101. With that said, it's one of the loveliest and most romantic drives if you have the time and patience.

Sales Tax
The state sales tax is 7.25%, and local taxes can be as much as 1.25%.

Smoking
You must be 18 to purchase tobacco products, and smoking is prohibited in all public buildings (including restaurants, bars and casinos) and enclosed spaces throughout California. It's also illegal to smoke within 20 feet of doorways or windows of government buildings. Many large hotels offer overnight accommodations for smokers, however, if you light up in a nonsmoking room you may be fined. The same rule applies with many rental car companies, too. Many cities in California have passed ordinances prohibiting smoking in all public places, including beaches. My advice: When in doubt, put it out.

Area Codes

Area code	Selected cities
408	San Jose
415	San Francisco, San Rafael
510	Oakland, Berkeley
650	Palo Alto, San Mateo
707	Napa/Sonoma, Mendocino, Ferndale
805	Cambria, San Simeon
831	Monterey, Carmel, Santa Cruz
530	Lake Tahoe
559	Yosemite
916	Sacramento

Telephone/Area Codes

The area code system isn't quite as confusing in the northern part of the state as it is in the Los Angeles area. For example San Francisco still has only one area code, 415, while Los Angeles has seven area codes with rumors of yet another split. See area codes sidebar on the previous page.

Time Zone

The entire state of California operates on Pacific Standard Time (Greenwich Mean Time minus eight hours) and trails three hours behind the East Coast. Daylight Savings Time is also observed.

Tipping

It is standard to tip between 15 to 20% at restaurants on the total bill for meals (before tax), and 10% at restaurants that offer counter service or buffet-style dining. An easy way to calculate 15% of the bill is to just double the sales tax. Taxis are 10%, valet is $2-3, bellhops receive 50 cents to $1 per bag, and maid service is $1-2 per day. If you receive exceptional service or someone goes above and beyond the call of duty, then a more generous tip may be warranted.

Tourist Information

The **California Department of Tourism** can supply you with information on the entire state as well as selected regions. You can obtain visitors' guides, brochures, maps, and special publications to help you better plan your trip. *Info*: www.visitcalifornia.com. Tel. 877/CALIFORNIA.

You can get a better sense of San Francisco and the rest of Northern California, including the Central Coast, by visiting the specific visitors bureaus of the cities profiled in this book – after all, they are the *best of* Northern California:
• Cambria Chamber of Commerce, Tel. 805/927-3624
• Ferndale Chamber of Commerce, Tel. 707/786-4477
• Lake Tahoe Visitors Authority, www.bluelaketahoe.com, Tel. 800/288-2463
• Mendocino County Alliance, www.gomendo.com, Tel. 866/466-3636
• Monterey County Convention & Visitors Bureau, www.montereyinfo.org, Tel. 831/657-6400

- Napa Valley Conference & Visitors Bureau, www.napavalley.org. Tel. 707/226-7459
- Napa-Sonoma Wine Country Visitor Services Center, Tel. 707/ 642-0686
- San Francisco Convention & Visitors Bureau, www.sfvisitor.org, Tel. 415/391-2000
- Santa Cruz County Conference & Visitors Council, www.santacruz.org, Tel. 831/425-1234
- Sonoma County Tourism Bureau, www.sonomacounty.com. Tel. 707/522-5800
- Yosemite Public Information Office, www.yosemite.com, Tel. 209/372-0200

INDEX

Things Change!

Phone numbers, prices, addresses, quality of service – all change. If you come across any new information, we'd appreciate hearing from you. No item is too small! Drop us an e-mail at jopenroad@aol.com, visit us at www.openroadguides.com, or write us at:

Open Road's Best of Northern California
Open Road Publishing
P.O. Box 284
Cold Spring Harbor, NY 11724

TRAVELNotes

TRAVELNotes

PHOTO CREDITS

ABOUT THE AUTHOR

Elizabeth Arrighi Borsting is a freelance writer and public relations consultant for the hospitality industry. Her writing credits include *Celebrity Weddings & Honeymoon Getaways, Open Road's Southern California Guide* (named first runner up for Best Travel Guide 2007 by the North America Travel Journalist Association), *California's Best B&Bs*, and *LA With Kids*. She served as a contributing editor for both *Honeymoon Magazine* and *Preferred Destinations*. Her work has also appeared in the *Los Angeles Times, National Geographic Traveler* and *OC Metro*. She resides with her husband Kurt and their two children, Jake and Katie, plus pup Ruby Jean, along the coast in Long Beach, California, just south of Los Angeles.

Open Road Publishing

Open Road has launched **a radical new concept in travel guides** that we call our *Best Of* guides: matching the time you *really* have for your vacation with the right amount of information you need for your perfect trip! No fluff, just the best things to do and see, the best places to stay and eat. Includes one-day, weekend, one-week and two-week trip ideas – in living color!

Best Of Guides

Open Road's Best of Arizona, $14.95
Open Road's Best of The Florida Keys, $14.95
Open Road's Best of Las Vegas, $14.95
Open Road's Best of New York City, $14.95
Open Road's Best of Southern California, $14.95
Open Road's Best of Belize, $14.95
Open Road's Best of Costa Rica, $14.95
Open Road's Best of Honduras, $14.95
Open Road's Best of Panama, $14.95
Open Road's Best of Ireland, $14.95
Open Road's Best of Italy, $16.95
Open Road's Best of Paris, $12.95
Open Road's Best of Provence &
    The French Riviera, $14.95
Open Road's Best of Spain, $14.95

Family Travel Guides

Open Road's Italy with Kids, $16.95
Open Road's Paris with Kids, $16.95
Open Road's Caribbean with Kids, $14.95
Open Road's London with Kids, $14.95
Open Road's New York City with Kids, $14.95
Open Road's Best National Parks With Kids, $12.95
Open Road's Washington, DC with Kids, $14.95
Open Road's Hawaii with Kids, $14.95

Eating & Drinking Guides

Eating & Drinking in Paris, $9.95
Eating & Drinking in Italy, $9.95
Eating & Drinking in Spain, $9.95

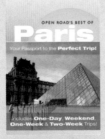